MY DIECAST LIFE

BY DAN VADO

My Die-Cast Life
isbn ISBN: 978-1-59362-330-2
Written By Dan Vado
www.danvado.com

Published by SLG Publishing
44 Race Street
San Jose, CA 95126
www.slgpubs.com

Instagram - slgpubs
Facebook - slgpublishing

My Die-Cast Life © 2025 Dan Vado
All rights reserved. No portion of this book may be reproduced, stored, or transmitted in any form or by any means—electronic, mechanical, photocopying, recording, mimeograph, or otherwise—without permission from the publisher, except for brief quotations in reviews or articles.

This is a work of memory, nostalgia, and imagination. The events and people described herein are drawn from real life but filtered through the author's recollections, embellishments, and sense of humor. Where necessary, names and details have been changed to protect both the innocent and the guilty.

Printed in The United States
 First Edition

CREDITS

Cover & Interior Illustrations

Deea Deac
@deeadraws

Additional Interior Illustrations

Jef Bambas
@ model_a_comic

Cover & Book Design

Scott Saavedra
@scottsaav

Editors

Jef Bambas
@ model_a_comic

Emily Parent
@indiesweetheartemily

Per la mamma e 'o Bobbo
con tutto l'amore di un figlio

Table of Contents

Introduction 1

Custom Barracuda 5

Red Baron 11

Johnny Lightning Topper Baja 12

The Heavyweights Tow Truck 13

Whip Creamer 15

Twin Mill 16

Paddy Wagon 18

Purple Lotus Turbine 20

Mighty Maverick 22

Custom Dodge Charger 25

Jet Threat 27

Custom Corvette 33

Python 36

Splittin' Image 41

Custom Barracuda 47

Part Two 47

Bubble Gunner 50

1978 50

Purple Funny Money 52

Beach Bomb 54

Maserati Mistral 56

Custom Camaro 60

Olds 442 66

1937 Bugatti 68

Custom Mustang 70

Ferrari 312P 74

Silhouette 77

Introduction
2025

If you bought this book expecting it to be about Hot Wheels cars, well, sorry. It isn't. You spent your money though, and I am not giving it back, so you may as well get a little into the book. What you hold in your hands is a brief series of vignettes from my life around 1968-1971, told through the lens of playing with toy cars and hanging out with my friends on Sunday afternoons. It is not a biography, but more of a glimpse of some parts of my life that were uniquely happy.

The genesis of this book was when I found a carrier full of Hot Wheels cars in my mom's attic while cleaning out her attic after she passed away. I had some fun looking at them and rolling them along the floor remembering the good times I had with them playing with my friends, but it was an odd look for someone in his sixties to be rolling toy cars across the floor. While the thought passed my mind to keep them, I was struggling with the idea of having fewer things in my life, not more. And so, to eBay they would go, hopefully to good homes with people who might appreciate them as much as I once did.

As I started putting together the first listing, I got to the part in the auction template where the description was supposed to go. In the box, there was this faint gray text that said: "Tell people about your item and why you are selling it." I figured that was a leftover from when eBay was mostly for people unloading household junk or random garage-sale stuff. But then it hit me—every

one of these cars actually had a little story behind it. So, instead of just writing something typical and conventionally descriptive, I started talking about what it was like playing with the car as a kid, or the memory it stirred up when I pulled it out again.

Pretty soon I was doing this for almost every listing, and the funny thing is, people started checking out my auctions just to read the stories.
Which brings me to the transparency portion of this introduction; how much truth is in these stories.

What you're about to read is based on real events. Some stories are told exactly as they happened, some are combined to create a fuller narrative, and a few are, admittedlly, slightly dramatized to make for better reading. All of the kids in these stories are based on my actual friends. One recurring character, Petra, is actually a combination of two girls I had crushes on in elementary school. The name comes from one of them, whose real name was so wholesome it almost didn't seem real. Some of the stories are exacly straight up what I put in the listings, while some of them have been expanded on to serve a greater narrative.

In the end I took in about $8500 from these cars, which is impressive until you consider that my mom, in her infinite wisdom, asked in her will that I send $10,000 to St. Jude. With no real direction on what she meant by that, I wound up sending the money to the Children's Hospital.

True story.

Custom Barracuda 1968

The year was 1968, or so. My mom was taking me on a trip to a local toy store; a wondrous, glorious, cavernous mecca of toys called Kiddie World. We weren't going to get toys, though. Kiddie World also sold swimming pool supplies, and my dad had just had an above-ground pool sunk into the ground in our back yard, so my mom, who had now become the primary caretaker of this folly of a swimming hole, was now given the responsibility of maintaining it. That meant buying chemicals and sweeping out the thousands of bugs that decided to breathe their last in our pool.

I knew the chances of my getting a new toy were slim, but just walking through Kiddie World was an experience that would leave any kid breathless, so I went along gladly and hoped that my mom might take pity on me and maybe reward me for my good behavior. I had once tried the "being a brat in the store until my mom bought me something" gambit and that wound up as such a memorable and spectacular failure that I learned to never push my mom's limits, in that way, ever again.

I loved toys, (what kid didn't?), but I what I really mean is: I LOOOVED TOYS. My favorite toys were the ones I could make my own adventures with. GI Joes, Captain Action, MAJOR MATT MASON! Don't even get me started on Major Matt Mason: a space toy line released in the 60s and designed to capitalize on the real-life space race. I could probably write half a book on Major Matt Mason and the moonscape I set up in the side yard of my house, where I ripped up something I thought were weeds to expose the dirt and make it look like a barren moonscape only to later discover it was something my mom had planted, probably zucchini. I got in big-time trouble and yelled at in two languages.

It took me a long time to want to eat zucchini again, but this is, of course, the first of what will be many digressions.

Anyway, to get to the pool section of Kiddie World, you had to walk past one of the larger toy aisles (these guys were not dummies) and, of course, my eyes darted around to see what was new. My mom was literally dragging me to the back of the store mumbling, "No toys. We gotta get da chlorine and da shock and da acid..."

She sounded like some sort of mad chemist who was going to create a gas creature in our pool that would devour the neighbors, whom, by the way, she swore up and down had killed our dog Lassie. She was so focused, looking at a list in her hand, that she let go of mine and let me wander freely through the giant aisle. My eyes started to dart around, losing track of my mom and looking at all the new toys that had just gone onto the shelves: GI Joes, Barbies, Green Army Men, Chatty Cathys, Outer Space Men. I had gotten blissfully lost in them all, thinking about the terrains and stories I could have with any of these toys in the now barren side yard (except for the Barbie because, well, because).

I'm not sure how long I wandered through the aisle, but it seemed like my mom had materialized from the back with a shopping cart filled with pool chemicals, nets, plastic hoses, and some giant brushes. Not a toy in the bunch.

"C'ma, we gotta go, da pool is green and you fadder wan' me to cook steak for some American friends."

By now you will have noticed a specific speech pattern from my mom, so this is where I tell you that I am a first-generation American. My parents were both immigrants coming here (separately) from Italy a few years after the end of World War II. My first language was Italian, and that's what we spoke at home for as far back as I can remember. Then one of my parents' immigrant friends—who also had a kid trying to learn English—told them that they needed to start speaking in English around the house or I was going to be at a disadvantage when I got to school. So overnight, my parents went all in. They spoke English to me, made me answer in English, and even told their friends they had to do the same around me. The plan was solid: get me ready for school so I could talk to teachers and be conversational with the other kids. In reality, the plan had flaws. It was like learning to play the piano from someone who doesn't have fingers – you might be able to play something, but it is not going to sound right. I found the most helpful thing at the time was watching TV and later translating soap operas for my grandmother, who absolutely refused to speak English.

Anyway, back at the toy aisle, I was standing in front of something I had never noticed before- a display of die-cast metal cars called Hot Wheels. They were cool, all muscle car looking, and sleek. Basically a 1/64th scale piece of something resembling freedom. I had a car in my hand, a Custom Barracuda. My eyes were wide; though this thing was still in the package and I had already mentally placed myself in the driver's seat of this sporty-looking car with red lines on the tires. The red lines I later learned were a big deal as they indicated that these came from the first 10 or so years of Hot Wheels production. Redline cars are highly prized by collectors.

I was still gazing at this car when my mom snatched it out of my hand and tossed it in the cart. It was amazing because I hadn't even asked her for it yet. That is when I noticed the extended packages of orange track that were stacked below the car display.

"We need this too…" I said, being ballsy and going for broke "… the car won't work without the track!" I said, figuring that if I believed it, so would she. Without hesitation, my mom grabbed the box of track and tossed it in the cart. This was easy, too easy I thought. I filed this strategy away for future use.

We got home and while my mom went straight to the back yard to mess with the pool, I went into the front room (that's what we called a rarely used living room with a hardwood floor and a mish-mash of semi-antique furniture that my Zia Elsa cast aside). I examined the box of track to figure out how to set it up. I didn't know about creating a ramp yet and just laid it out flat so it created an orange expressway between the couch and a recliner. I took the Barracuda out of its package, put it at one end of the track, and gave it a push. I added a sound effect as it rolled to the other end of the track seemingly on its own power.

"ZOOOOOOOMMMMM!"

The Barracuda got to the end of the track, hopped off, and continued in a straight line until it hit the front door and in that moment, I was transformed. The sight of how easily this car glided along its track, the determined way it rolled off the track and kept going, stopping only until it hit a wall, was like nothing I had ever seen before. This car was no mere toy; it was all the possible futures I might have—a car, a BOSS car, one that almost drove itself. I heard my mom stirring in the kitchen, having finished whatever swimming pool alchemy she had been working on.

"Company comn'. Pick dis up and put it away!" she commanded. Having learned the hard way what could happen if I left my toys out when company came over, I snapped to it and hustled my newfound favorite toy ever into my room, planning my next move to get more cars and more track.

Monday rolled around, and I decided I was going to show off this new coolest thing ever to my friends. I grabbed the Barracuda and stuffed it into my pocket, figuring I would show it off at lunch to my friends, who would always marvel at the food I brought to school because it was filled with cured meats and delicacies that they would never see in their own homes. A salami sandwich was nothing compared to a nicely made mortadella and mozzarella sandwich with oil, vinegar, and tomatoes. My mom worked in an Italian market, (well, it was just a market in an Italian neighborhood), so my lunches looked like they came from the best restaurant in the city. Growing up I took prosciutto and melon for granted and was stunned how much of a delicacy it seemed like to my friends.

So lunchtime comes around and my friends, gathered around me to see what I had in my bag, were sizing me up for a possible trade. Moorpark Elementary School had a time-honored lunch swap ritual where kids traded lunches just to escape the monotony of eating the same thing every day. Everyone knew that there was no way I was trading my coppocola and ricotta sandwich with lettuce, tomato, and an olive oil drizzle for a PB& J. I once tried trading, just to make friends, but I immediately regretted it and never did it again.

So, to get their minds off my sandwich, I pulled the Barracuda out of my pocket. "Look what I got on Saturday…"

"Hey, Hot Wheels!" interrupted my friend Michael, a big kid who was sometimes my best friend, "Nice- a Barracuda!"

I was a little surprised. I thought I had discovered this all on my own, but soon found out that I was the one who was late to the party as people gathered around to talk about the cars they owned, and which ones they might one day like to drive, and also how Hot Wheels were WAY better than Matchbox cars.

"This one really moved down the track I set up..." I didn't even get a chance to finish my sentence when a noticeable murmur swept over my friends.

"Track?" Michael asked, "You have track?"

"Yeah, my mom bought it for me when..."

"Your mom bought you track? And she let you set it up?"

"Uh, yeah...why?"

"My mom wouldn't let me set up the track in our house because she said it would ruin the floor."

I could see my mom saying the same thing, but she was more obsessed with the swimming pool that day and perhaps didn't think the normal mom thoughts when I started playing with a die-cast car in the living room. The bell sounded, signaling the end of lunchtime, and as we walked back to class, someone asked, "Hey, can I come run my cars on your track sometime?"

Now, I did not have a ton of close friends other than Michael in school at that time, and they were all, for one reason or another, a little afraid of my mom.

"Yeah, maybe you guys could come over on Sunday after church, and I could get my mom to make us some snacks." I can not stress enough that, regardless of whatever fear my friends had of my mom, they had a healthy respect for what that woman could do with a snack tray, so of course they were all excited to come to my house on a Sunday and race their cars. And thus was born what I would call "The Maywood Avenue Sunday Race Car Derby and Lunch Jamboree."

Now all I had to do was get my mom to buy me more track, more cars...

... and make lunch.

Red Baron
1969

Looking back, I don't know who the Hot Wheels Red Baron car was meant for. Featuring a World War I infantry-style helmet with an Iron Cross emblazoned on its sides, at the time, I thought this was supposed to be a nod to the famous flying ace, the Red Baron, brought to life for most of us by Snoopy in the Peanuts cartoons. In his World War I Flying Ace daydreams, Snoopy would chase the Red Baron with his "Sopwith Camel" (which was really just his doghouse, with him perched on top wearing aviator goggles). As far as I know, Snoopy never caught the Red Baron, but every kid, or at least every kid I knew, would yell "Curse you, Red Baron!" at the top of their lungs while shaking a fist (or paw) in mock outrage just like Snoopy.

This car suddenly appeared in my collection; a present from my mom who must have thought it was what I was screaming at the air about. It did well on the living room track, but never made it to my Sunday competition use, which explains why the paint is in such great shape. When I won with it, though, everyone would shout "CURSE YOU RED BARON!" at the top of their lungs.

By the time I recovered this 50 years later, the helmet showed some years of tarnish. I could have probably rubbed it off, but I was afraid to take off the iron cross. Given that I was currently sporting a fair bit of tarnish myself at this point in my life I figured this was representative of my own life's path.

More or less.

Johnny Lightning Topper Baja 1970

Occasionally my mom, who really did not know the difference, would bring a car that was NOT a Hot Wheels into the mix. The Johnny Lightning brand of cars were designed to compete with Hot Wheels both in the marketplace and in the 1/64 track that was in my living room.

This thing definitely looked the part: two engines- one in the front, one in the back, with a total of 16 exhaust pipes coming out of the side. Two eight-cylinder, high-perfomance engines plopped into this thing with a cockpit in the middle where the driver would sit and, presumably, become deaf from sitting between them. The cockpit driver area was something of a common theme in this type of imaginary car, like a drag racer or maybe a place for the pilot of a flightless plane. The existence of this cabin made the car seem fast and, if it existed in the real world, dangerous to drive.

Some people claimed that the Johnny Lightning cars were faster than Hot Wheels. Though I had my doubts, I eagerly anticipated bringing this into the Sunday afternoon Maywood Avenue race competition and pizza party.

This car actually did turn in some impressive times in test sprints. However, the panel of judges, which was really just my across-the-street neighbor's cousin's best friend who we HAD to have along because she had nothing to do on Sundays since her mom drank and her dad had a "special friend" that he would go to see after church and if she DIDN'T come along then her brother and cousin would have to take her to the park and we would be short of the quorum needed to get the races started, all she could bring herself to say on the matter was "It's NOT a Hot Wheels" and that was enough to earn a DQ for this car and for the Johnny Lightning brand as a whole.

So we will never truly know how The Baja held up against the competition. I wound up listing the car as "used" due to its age, but it reality it never hit the orange track in a competitive way and now only serves as a reminder that life is not fair

The Heavyweights Tow Truck 1969

The Heavyweight Tow Truck was an important part of my Hot Wheels test track on Maywood Avenue despite the fact that it never saw any actual time on the track itself. This vehicle was the major first responder to ANY accident that occurred on my living room raceway. Its major asset being that it could actually tow ANY Hot Wheels car. If one of the racers flew off the track, I would hitch them up to the tow truck and haul them to the back of the line where I, as the race marshall and whose mom was supplying lunch to a bunch of hungry, poorly fed Americans, would determine if the car could race again that day or if it needed to "convalesce".

I was obsessed with the word convalesce because a skilled nursing facility had opened up the street from my house and I rode my bike past it on Saturday afternoons to get cheeseburgers at this small burger stand that made my favorite burgers before McDonald's came along and changed everything. The sign outside the place read "Something Something Convalenscent Hospital." One day on my way to the burger place I spotted a nurse coming out so I rode over to her and asked her what a convalescent hospital was.

"It's a place you go to get better, I hope you NEVER have to come here."

From that day forward all cars that jumped the track were forced to convalesce, which was my way of showing off that I knew a fancy word.

This habit of mine created stress in my beloved Maywood Avenue Sunday Pizza Party and Sprint Car Rally Club. I was the only one that really wanted the towing of wrecked cars to become ritualistic, everyone else just wanted to race and eat snacks. But, without tradition and ritual are we not just savages? Do we not want to care about the items we fling down the plastic raceway? Should we not rest until we are better? According to my fellow racers, no.

Whatever.

Regardless of what you think about this as a collector's item (or as my Italian mom would put it 'a collectum' item') everyone should have a tow truck as part of their Hot Wheels menagerie. A silent, green sentinel standing at the ready for all disasters.

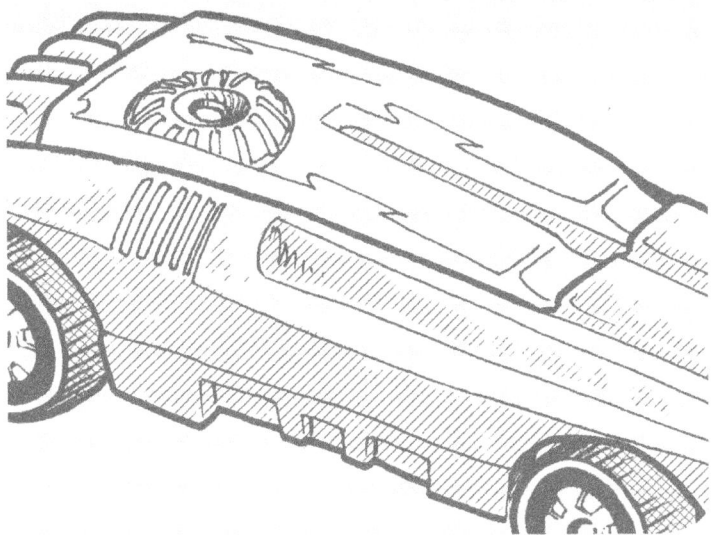

Whip Creamer
1970

The 1969 Hot Wheels Whip Creamer in metallic gold, (or pukey yellow), take your pick. An unfortunately named car which had the capability of being a real contender on Sunday afternoon in the Maywood Avenue Invitationals. Maybe the only thing holding it back was the name. Any time, and EVERY time, I dragged it out to race the inevitable childish chorus of "Whip Creamer man, bring out your whip cream! Are you going to play with your whip creamer?" would start.

The childishness of the whole thing was to be expected, us being children and all. More to the point though was that most of us, probably none of us, really understood the meaning of our taunts. The car was fast, very aero-dynamic, and flew down that orange track at speeds matched only by my beloved Silhouette. But that name! It was the name. It was just not a name that you would bestow on any true racer. I can still hear it. "Hey, look at little Danny pulling out his Whip Creamer! "

Nobody needs that at age ten.

So, to avoid the taunting I kept my Whip Creamer hidden and only played with it when I was alone.

It was a boss car though, it was fast and had a lot going for it.

Twin Mill
1969

Somewhere in my mind there exists a movie script that features characters who live in the Hot Wheels universe. The storyline was of course born on Maywood Avenue when my friends and I raced our cars on Sunday afternoon and we would get to talking about the cars and who would actually drive any of these.

My friend Karl across the street's favorite car was The Twin Mill.

"Two engines for smoking you like my dad's Camels" he would say. We all made fun of him; why would two small engines be better than one big one? Mind you none of us, well, almost none of us, knew anything about real cars or their engines so maybe two engines WERE better than one...

Whatever, Karl used to beat our asses on the regular with his Twin Mill, and yet, the more he beat us the more we made fun of him. For his part, Karl took it all in stride. Of all my friends Karl was probably the smartest. Not just book smart, but he seemed wise beyond his years and he was not someone who was going to let being taunted by us drag him down.

Until the day he actually got into his dad's Camels and his mom grounded him for six months and took away his cars. I rescued his Twin Mill from the church's charity bin and tried to give it back to him but no, he was now done with Hot Wheels and decided that I should keep his prized car as well as the trophy case version (the one I am selling today) because I was the only one who had been honest enough to give him his car back.

But here I have to come clean: the person he should really have thanked was my mom because SHE was the one who made me give the car back after discovering what had happened. I would have kept it and was in the process of working up an story for why I had a Twin Mill car of the same color with the same scratches as his champion.

I feel bad to this day. Not everything on Maywood Ave had a happy ending.

Paddy Wagon
1969

A paddy wagon, if you're not familiar with the term, is what people called police vans that carted around those who had been arrested back in the 19th century, and hauling them off as a group to a local jail. The term has a derogatory, racist origin, as "Paddy" was what the uptight racists of that era would call Irish people- most specifically men. It was a take on the name Patrick, which was common in Irish culture. In its original usage in the U.K., the vehicle was called a Patty Wagon and may have become Paddy Wagon here in the U.S., with its original intent being lost in translation.

It's a little off-putting as I look at this toy with my 21st-century eyes and think that I would never in a million years have bought—or kept—a toy called a Wop Wagon, but here it was, in my collection of toys. And back in the day, when I didn't know any better, I would play with this thing without giving it a second thought.

Honestly, I never raced with it, and just looking at the car—why would you even think to? Square and boxy and not the least bit aerodynamic, it seemed like something you'd never expect to stand up against a Corvette or a Charger. So instead, this vehicle stood sentry as security during the Maywood Avenue Sunday Invitationals and Hot Dog Roast, keeping the imaginary crowd in line. We all just sort of forgot about it—until one day, a nice kid who lived on a different street, picked up my Paddy Wagon and said, "Isn't this thing supposed to take people off to jail?"

A murmur of "no duh" swept across my living room as we were simply annoyed with the question.

"If that's the case," he said, "why doesn't this one have a door on the back?"

That got everyone's attention. I assumed mine had fallen off due to neglect, but everyone who had one with them immediately pulled out their Paddy Wagon, and indeed, none of them had a door. This thing, as a law enforcement vehicle, was apparently useless—beyond an albatross—and had now gone from being just a stupid car, to being an albatross with a badge. Away mine went, given that its one purpose—to restore order in a chaotic climate—had now been tossed, against the logic of a ten-year-old.

Later, my sixth-grade teacher (who was Irish) would tell us the meaning of the word Paddy, and from then on I felt sort of bad. Later in the school year he would taunt me for being Italian, and all of those warm feelings of sympathy went away.

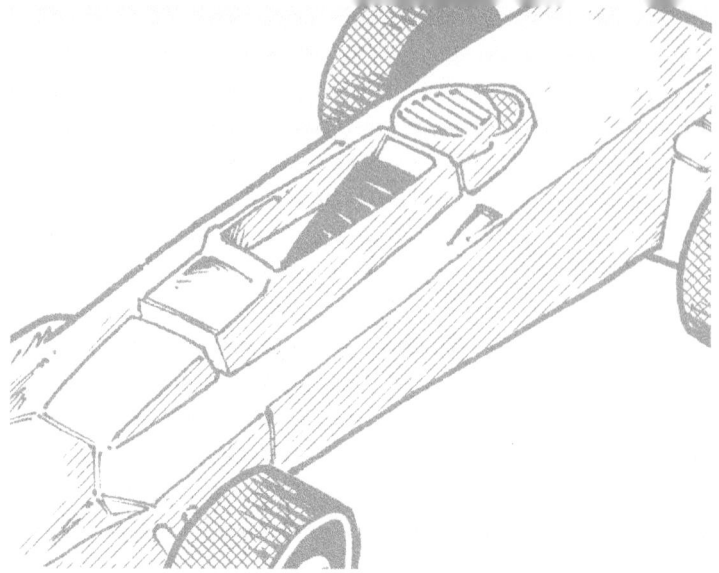

Purple Lotus Turbine
1969

This was another one of the star cars at the Sunday Afternoon Maywood After-Church Invitational. It was called an Invitational because there was a kid down the street who was a creep that gave off negative waves and quite possibly was eating his own boogers (according to well founded rumors) so, to get into my house you needed an invitation because my mom did not tolerate booger eaters.

This car would fly down that orange track at speeds rarely seen, and it almost never wiped out — even on my cousin's crappy setup, which he built in the driveway as a way of trying to compete with our indoor Invitational. (Oh yeah, my cousin wasn't invited either.)

The Lotus's performance on the orange track was the complete opposite of the car it was based on — the 1968 Lotus 56, which featured a fuel-injected turbine engine and four-wheel drive. Two of the three Lotus cars entered in the Indy 500 that year failed to finish due to mechanical issues with the fuel injection, and the third one crashed. Later, a fourth car also crashed — this time killing its driver.

Not satisfied and still hoping to build a car that could at least finish a race, Lotus redesigned one of the wrecked cars and re-entered it. The new version, however, was bloated, slow, underpowered, and overweight — a sad, lumbering version of a dream that ended in disappointment.

All of which, of course, we didn't know or care about on Maywood Avenue. We read something about the Lotus once during an Indy 500 broadcast and decided that maybe all the designer really needed to do was invent a giant orange track that started at the top of a couch or dining room table and ended in a crash zone of gargantuan pillows. No engine required — just gravity. Pretty simple really.

Later, we would go on to figure out how to end the war in Vietnam and make beer taste more like soda.

Kids have the answers to everything.

Mighty Maverick
1969

This car was in excellent condition when I found it. It was rarely raced, and other than some slight discoloration in the paint (which I assume is just age — honestly, everything from 1969 should look this good), the wheels spin great and it drives in a nice straight line!

But of course, there's a story behind why this car was rarely raced and why it's in such great shape.

I acquired it on one of my jaunts to the local neighborhood toy store (Kiddie World — I miss you). Upon taking it out of its package, I was convinced this was the fastest Hot Wheels ever made. So convinced, in fact, that I marched straight down to my friend Chewie's house to prove it. (We called him Chewie because, well, I guess his real name was hard for kids with braces and missing teeth to pronounce. A few years later when Star Wars came out, Chewie stopped coming around altogether — he knew he was in for it.)

Anyway, Chewie had a ventriloquist dummy in his closet that belonged to his older brother, who was living in Canada for exactly the reason any older teen would move to Canada in 1969. I was obsessed with that dummy and was utterly convinced that if I had it, I'd become the next great comedian-slash-ventriloquist to guest star on The Merv Griffin Show!

Chewie was pretty much done with the dummy — his brother hadn't written in a while, and the thing was taking up space where he wanted to store his baseball gear. He hadn't been able to trade it for anything of real value because his asking price was always "one of your mom's bras," which was a place nobody wanted to go with Chewie.

So I went down to his house and offered him this most badass Hot Wheels car in trade for the doll. Chewie took one look at the car, looked back at me, and said, "DEAL!"

I grabbed the doll and bolted out the door, figuring I'd gotten the better end of it and should probably get home before his mom jumped in to overturn the trade. (Because of past bad toy swaps, the moms in our neighborhood had agreed that any trade could be revoked with a simple phone call from one mom to another.)

I named my new doll Mr. Willowbottoms and marched straight into the kitchen to show my mom what I could do by having Mr. Willowbottoms tell her a joke.

"HEY MOM!" I yelled. "MEET MR. WILLOWBOTTOMS!" Then I launched into my act.

"Mmy drd da cjkkn csss ma rrrruud?"

My mom stared at me and the dummy and said, "What da hell dat is?"

"He's Mr. Willowbottoms, my ventriloquist doll! I'm going to be a great ventriloquist like Edgar Bergen on The Ed Sullivan Show!"

The Ed Sullivan Show was one of her favorites, and we'd watch it together on Sunday nights after dinner and before bed (for me, anyway).

"More like Charlie McCarthy," my mom replied. I didn't realize until later that she was making a joke at my expense — Charlie McCarthy was the dummy. Nice one, Mom. I never knew she had it in her.

She rolled her eyes in that way only she could and asked, "Where'd you get it?"

So I told her that I'd traded my new Hot Wheels car to Chewie for it — and I swear, I had barely gotten his name out of my mouth before she was on the phone with Chewie's mom, canceling the deal.

I had to slink back to his house and get my car back.

So ashamed was I by the whole incident that I never brought the car out again. I later heard that Chewie's mom ended up burning the dummy because of all the trades she had to intervene in — and because she was tired of having to explain the "bra thing" over and over again.

Anyway, I never became a famous ventriloquist or a comedian, but I did write comic books for a while. Almost the same thing.

So, you know — I've got that going for me.

Custom Dodge Charger 1968

This is not a story about the Maywood Ave Sunday Race and Pizza Party, or a story of he-man-woman-haters or anything else like that. This is the story of loyalty to one's father as well as not being able to tell one color from the other.

The 1968 Custom Dodge Charger showed up in my collection one day after one of my Saturday afternoon tantrums where my mom figured only a trip to Kiddie World for a new toy car would settle me down. (Yes, I was a brat, why do you think I have so many of these cars?)

Anyway, the Charger in Lime (or metallic or anti-freeze) green was the only one of it's kind on the hook. I made my mom buy it and took it home and tore it out the package. I rolled it across the kitchen table and, while a little heavy, I figured it would make for a good racer, and for a car that would get Petra (you remember Petra right? More on her later.) to talk to me at school.

It was then that my dad strode into the kitchen. He looked at me playing with the Charger and asked me what kind of car it was.

"Dodge Charger" I replied gleefully.

My dad scowled. He looked down at me and the car and said "Only crooks drive Chargers" and then he went into the living room and did not speak a single word to me until Sunday. The car bugged him and clearly even nine-year-old selfish brat me could see that he did not like seeing it. Today we would say he was triggered. Back then we said he was just irritable.

At any rate, I put the car away and never, and I mean NEVER, brought it out again, Which is why it is in such great shape.

As for the color part of the story, try as I can I am not sure what to call this color, It is a shiny metallic green for sure.

Would I call it Lime? Yeah, I would.

Would I call it Anti-freeze? Maybe.

I have seen these green chargers described in many a different way. So for auction purposes let's just call it metallic, which I am positive is an accurate description.

Jet Threat
1971

The Jet Threat. Ah, now that was a car of dreams and adventures. While I liked the Hot Wheels that were miniature versions of real cars, my favorites were always the ones born from pure fantasy — and the Jet Threat was certainly one of those.

This car, I imagined, was supposed to be a dragster — something meant to sprint at inhuman speeds down a test track and then slow by way of a parachute that would pop out the back, allowing it to decelerate enough for the driver to apply brakes without going through the windshield.

Smack dab in the middle of the car sat a giant jet engine — or what I could only assume was one — something big enough to push a fighter plane through the sky. A massive intake turbine dominated the front, and the rear had two big exhausts for air to move through. A cockpit-style cabin sat at the back of the car, giving the driver a view over the roaring engine.

Pure fantasy, of course; sadly no real-life vehicle that this was based on, but in my head a car like this had to exist somewhere out there. And much like my beloved Camaro, I was sure I'd one day own my own Jet Threat and drive it around the school parking lot, setting the grass field on fire with the super-heated exhaust as revenge for having spent hours in detention for playing with the sprinklers in that same field — pretending they were machine guns shooting down imaginary Fokker triplanes from World War I as I screamed "CURSE YOU, RED BARON!" at the top of my lungs. That little performance led to a teacher suggesting I could "use a little time with the school counselor," but it was instead decided that I'd spend all my recesses for a week in Miss Bruno's classroom (the only teacher in my elementary school with a vowel at the end of her name), staring at my desk and writing, "I will not play with the sprinklers shooting down imaginary German planes and damaging school property." Every day I had to present the sheet to the head groundskeeper, who would take it, rip it in half, and bark, "AGAIN!"

But I digress.

The Jet Threat had all the makings of a racer that could melt the plastic track at the Maywood Avenue Sunday Pre-Dinner Drag Racing Invitational. For whatever reason, though, it was middling — it didn't win much and looked cooler than it performed. Still, I'd always bring it out and display it to my friends, usually setting it on the table that served as the staging area for the Sunday races.

One day I was setting up the track when my friend Michael from up the block wandered in with his box of cars. He went straight to the staging table, took a deep sniff of whatever my mom was cooking for Sunday dinner and then started unpacking his cars. That's when he spotted the Jet Threat sitting in the middle.

"Not this piece of junk," Michael said. He was not a fan, though he wasn't really a fan of anything.

Michael and I were in the same grade, but he was two years older — and somehow older than his "twin" sister, who was actually my age. I later learned they'd been adopted, and for some reason their parents decided to call them twins. My personal theory was that they wanted him to look out for his sister in school. His sister Cindy was a handful; even in fifth grade she looked like a biker chick.

Because of his age, Michael was bigger than the rest of us and had a huskier voice. He also swore a lot. That combination made him a little intimidating. When I say he said, "Not this piece of junk," what he actually said was, "Not this piece of shit again." Michael commanded attention when he swore — which is probably why he did it so often. We all wondered why his parents never punished him for it. Were they afraid of him? Did swearing make you cool?

I wouldn't know. I'd get in trouble just for sounding like I was swearing. And when your parents don't speak English very well, the last thing you want is to mumble something and have one of them appear from nowhere demanding, "WHAT DAT MEAN?"

Most people are surprised when I tell them I'm a non-native English speaker and that my first language was Italian. I learned to fake fluency early — losing my accent and pronouncing words correctly made it sound like I understood better than I actually did. But non-native speakers have blind spots, and mine were irony and sarcasm.

Which brings us back to Michael and the Jet Threat. He was turning it over, looking for flaws and ways to make fun of me.

"What do you suppose the threat is?" he said. "Is it the jet?"

My parents had a strategy for situations they didn't fully understand — stay quiet and hope context eventually made sense. I hadn't learned that yet.

"Huh?" I said, looking at him for clarity, probably making myself sound dumb.

"You know," he continued, "is the car the threat, or just the jet? Why's it supposed to be so threatening?"

I still didn't get that he was just mocking the name. "It's just what they called it."

"Yeah, but what's the deal? Is the car the threat? Is it to jets? What?"

"Uh..." was all I could manage.

Michael put the car down. Now I was the focus. "You do speak English, right? I've heard you say actual words before."

I didn't like people mocking how I spoke, but I also didn't want things to escalate — I'd seen him beat up an eighth-grader once.

"What?" was my brave retort.

"It's a simple question!" he yelled. "Is it a threat because of the jet? Was it already a threat and now it's a Jet Threat? Is it a threat to jets?"

Now he was standing over me, swearing up a storm — which unfortunately caught the wrong person's attention.

My mom, Inez Vado, had entered the chat.

"What going on here? You fighting?"

Michael spun around and froze. "Uh…?"

My mom stepped into the room. Both of us gulped. She'd lived through World War II — or, as she called it, "Da Worl' War Secon'." She'd lost both parents, been abandoned by her sisters, and spent the rest of the war in a convent where nuns handled "time of the month" issues by locking girls in closets.

She did not understand irony or sarcasm and had zero tolerance for anyone making fun of me or anyone in the family.

"If you gonna fight, den you can go home," she told Michael.

"Uh…" he stammered, turning to me for help.

"I no wanna hear no more shitty language from you," she added, staring him down.

Everything I know about irony, I learned from my mom — mostly by watching her. She was an immigrant who thought there were too many foreigners in America (a common theme, I'd learn). She hated swearing, punished me for it constantly, yet cursed like a sailor when the mood struck her. Once, years later, she caught me on the phone in my office unloading on a vendor who'd been jerking me around. I hung up, furious, and she fixed me with that famous glare.

"Why you gotta talk like dat? You can't talk like dat in a business! WHERE DA HELL YOU GET DAT SHITTY LANGUAGE?"

Gee, Mom, I wonder.

Anyway — back to the scene. You could slice the tension with a cheap plastic spoon. I was relieved to no longer be Michael's target, but nobody on Earth knew better than I did how unpredictable my mother could be.

"S-sorry, Mrs. Vado," Michael muttered, eyes down.

Not satisfied, she issued the worst punishment available in our house on a Sunday.

"You no get no pizza," she declared, and marched back to the kitchen.

With the Jet Threat debate unresolved and the humiliation of no pizza hanging over him, Michael gathered his cars and left. My friends, arriving just as he was leaving, asked why. His only explanation: "No pizza for me." Everyone understood, and the rest of us were on our best behavior for the rest of the afternoon.

As for the Jet Threat — honestly, I still don't know what the big deal about the name was. Michael came back on other Sundays and always ate whatever was served, but he never mentioned the Jet Threat again, and he never made eye contact with my mom.

And like all epic tales, this one has a coda.

Not long after the incident, my Jet Threat went missing. It wasn't in my carrier, my track box, or mixed in with my other toy sets. I was deep into a Major Matt Mason adventure in the side yard and vaguely remembered thinking the Jet Threat could make a cameo — but it was the wrong scale, so I'd rejected the idea. The only conclusion was that someone had taken it, by accident or on purpose.

I suspected Michael — maybe some weird revenge on my mom. But when I asked, his denial was convincing. "Why the hell would I want that car?" Given his PTSD from being yelled at by my mom, I believed him.

Then, a few weeks later, a quiet kid named Mario — who lived across the street from Michael and was also first-gen kid — suddenly showed up with the exact same car in the exact same color, with the same perfectly placed stickers. It had to be mine. I was going to tell my mom, but thought better of it. If I was wrong, it would start an entirely new kind of hell: a chorus of Italian immigrants accusing each other of having "shitty sons" and being either bad Italians or too American (as if nobody ever stole anything in Italy — half the wartime economy was based on taking things from people).

My parents liked Mario's family — even though everyone was from Calabria, which my dad had very little patience for. They especially liked his sister Angela and thought she'd make a good match for me someday. With all that baggage, I decided to let it go. The car wasn't a true racer anyway, and I didn't need the reminder of how easily my mom could blow up over the smallest things. I never invited Mario over again, though, because deep down I still thought he was a little thief.

Flash forward half a century. I'm cleaning out stuff from my old room — a place I hadn't really touched since I was eighteen — and there it was. Top drawer of an old wooden dresser, buried behind worthless baseball cards: the Jet Threat. It hadn't been stolen. I'd either misplaced it or my mom had stuffed it away without telling me.

Decades later, I realized Mario wasn't a thief.

I never saw or spoke to him much after elementary school, even though he lived right up the street. I don't know where he ended up in life, but if he ever reads this book, I hope he knows I regret the assumption.

Also, Mario — you'd never have wanted me to marry your sister.

Custom Corvette 1968

I would assume that if you owned an actual Corvette, it would be the most prized thing in your life that wasn't alive. The Corvette wasn't just a car — it wasn't just an American car or a muscle car — it was a symbol of American performance and ingenuity. Coming into its own as a response to the European sports car, the Corvette evolved from concept car to sports car to muscle car, eventually earning the name Sting Ray because of its sleek design and contours.

The die-cast version was no different. The 1968 Custom Corvette was one of the first sixteen cars manufactured by Mattel — often referred to as the Original Sixteen or Sweet Sixteen. None of which mattered to us kids at the time, of course. When I first saw it, the Corvette was just a car hanging on a hook in a plastic clamshell package — one I made my mom buy on one of her many trips to Kiddie World for pool supplies.

The Corvette did not disappoint. It was aerodynamic, sleek, and cool-looking, and even though it was probably no faster than any of the other cars I owned, somehow it looked faster. In my mind it became a blur as it streaked down the track from the top of the dining-room table to the end of the line and into the couch cushions we used to soften the impact.

No one seemed to like the Corvette more than Petra, a cute blonde girl who lived in a cul-de-sac around the corner from my house. Petra was my age and had been in every one of my classes from first grade on. Her mom was nice enough — though my mom didn't like her much (no surprise there because my) — and her dad was a mechanic who often fixed cars for people in the neighborhood.

My dad was a TV repairman, so he and Petra's dad often traded services. In the 1960s, TVs seemed less reliable than cars — running a vacuum cleaner too close to the set could make the image wiggle, so we were regularly visiting Petra's house before dinner to restore the picture. Don't even get me started on when color TVs came along and everyone had to have one. My dad became the most popular man on the block — and probably regretted encouraging everyone to swap out their black-and-white sets for the latest color models.

Petra was closer to her dad than her mom and would often hang around him while he worked on cars. As a result, she developed an early familiarity with engines and body styles and was starting to know what was what in the automobile world. She was enamored with my Custom Corvette and swore up and down that one day she'd drive one in real life.

While she wasn't a regular at the Sunday Invitationals on Maywood, she'd sometimes wander over to watch the races when her parents told her to "go play with your friends." That phrase, as all of us neighborhood kids knew, was really code for "leave the house for a couple of hours so Mom and Dad can", as my mom would say, "do the rosary."

One Sunday afternoon, Petra showed up when only a couple of the guys were over. She went to say hi to my mom and told her she was there to "play with her friends," to which my mom responded, "Eh... huh... okay."

I was just pulling out my Corvette when Petra came back, and I could see how fixated she was on it. I placed the car at the top of the track, making small talk while trying to convince my friends not to bail just because a girl was in the house. I let the Corvette go, and Petra's eyes followed it like lasers. The car became a blur, hit the pillows at the end of the track with a soft thud, and she ran to retrieve it.

She looked at me and said, "I'm going to have one of these one day."

I thought she meant the toy — and since I had two of them, I said something stupid like, "Now you don't have to wait," and handed it to her. She smiled, checked the time, slipped the car into her pocket, and went off to someone else's house — or maybe home; I'm not sure which.

Later that week, Petra's dad brought the car back to my dad. Her parents told her to stop talking to me until they could "have a discussion" with mine. To this day, I have no idea what that was about.

Anyway, this car is great.

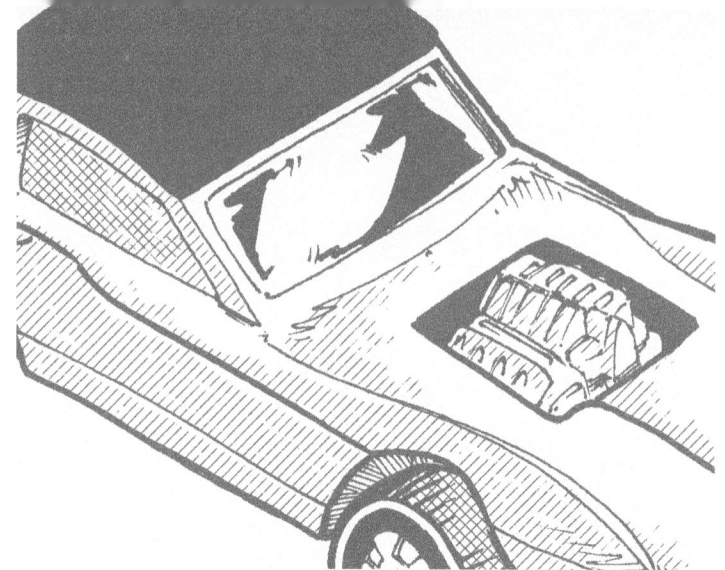

Python
1967

The Red 1967 Python — now that was a fast car and easily one of the best in my fleet. I won many a race on Sunday afternoons at the Maywood Invitational and Trash-Talking Contest. It was a tough car, but alas, the roof could not survive my stupidity.

Allow me to explain.

It rains in California on rare occasions, and it always seemed to rain on a Saturday afternoon, blowing up my plans to be anywhere but inside. My mom, for her part, would say this was a good opportunity to catch up on homework, clean my room, or go down to my dad's TV shop and have lunch with him.

I generally liked hanging out at my dad's shop on a Saturday. He didn't take being open that day too seriously and never seemed to put much effort into the random customer who might wander in. I think he preferred puttering around, getting the place ready for the week, and just hanging out.

He had an odd assortment of friends who would drop by — all of them Italian. And by Italian, I mean Italian-Italian: born in the old country, came here after the war, and now spent their days complaining that America was going to hell because of all the immigrants. They spoke English with heavy accents which, to me, didn't sound like accents at all; it was just how English sounded. Still, out of deference to my English-learning, my dad asked his friends to speak English when I was around.

Later, I came to realize that my mom was not the most stable of people, and that the shop was my dad's sanctuary, so when his friends came by, it was his version of a Hot Wheels club — a few guys sitting around, eating, talking, laughing.

My dad kept olive oil, anchovies, and assorted spices in the back. He loved taking some sourdough bread that was about to go stale, laying slices of tomato and anchovy on top, drizzling it with olive oil and oregano, letting it soak, and then cutting it up for lunch. I loved that dish — still do, when I can find good tomatoes.

When his buddies gathered, he'd put out his own buffet — sometimes pizza from a friend's restaurant up the street, sometimes leftovers from the night before (which was always fish, and maybe didn't keep as well as he thought). They'd show up around 11:30, set up in the back of the store, and rearrange his work tables into a makeshift bar. This was the 1960s, so a TV might be on showing a western or whatever movie was playing on the local UHF channels. My dad loved John Wayne movies; he could go on for hours about why Red River was such a great film. Mostly, though, they ignored the TV and talked about the old country and their wives — mostly complaints about both.

He was happiest in those moments, surrounded by his friends, eating and laughing. I rarely saw him angry with them — he seemed to save all that up for my mom. It was nice to see him content, which wasn't often when he was home.

Whenever I showed up at the shop, the greetings began.

"Ey, ciao, Dani! How you do'?" Stuff like that — cheerful but superficial. I never knew if they actually cared how I was, so I just smiled a lot.

"Whey, Arna', teach you boy some manners — he no answer when I talk to him!"

So, first off, my dad's name was Arnaldo. His Italian friends called him Arna', which he preferred over the Americanized "Arnie." Second, I didn't talk much with these guys because any conversation usually ended with my feelings hurt and my dad getting mad — at them, at me, or both. This rainy Saturday would be no different.

One of my dad's greasier friends was Nicola — everyone called him Nick. He always smelled like too much aftershave and had hair so slicked back it looked like a solid mass of shiny goop. Nick had daughters roughly my age, and I think he was constantly sizing me up as potential husband material. I had no idea how he thought he could determine that when I was still a kid, but I played along because my dad liked him.

I walked into the shop, dripping from the rain, went straight to the back where the repair area was, hung up my jacket, and pulled the Python out of my pocket. My mom had just bought it for me the day before because I'd helped her put away the dishes all week without complaining or breaking anything.

Yeah, low bar, I know.

Anyway, I went to my dad's workbench to play with my car and wait for lunch when Nick came over and asked, "What's that?"

"A car," I said quietly, hoping that would be the end of it. Nick reeked of Aqua Velva and whatever glue-like substance held his dyed jet-black hair in place — just talking to him made my eyes water.

"I know it's a car. What kind of car?"

"A Hot Wheels Python. It's new. This one's red!" I held it up to prove it. The Python, I later learned, was modeled after a custom car called The Cheetah, with long exhaust pipes and an exposed engine. Both were two-seat hot rods with angular bodies and, in my case, a black top.

"Why it have a black top? Is it a convertible?" Nick asked, apparently sincere.

"Uh, I don't think so." Most convertible toy cars I'd seen either had the top down or a removable roof. This was a hardtop — definitely not removable.

"Is it red under the black?"

"I dunno," I said. But the question stuck in my head.

"You don't know anything," Nick sneered. Then, without waiting for an answer, he turned to my dad. "Arna', you boy — you let him be 'Mericano. He's stupid.

He eat hot dogs instead of pizza. He no play calcio. He not even gonna marry an Italian girl!"

It was harsh, even for Nick — but it was a sentiment I'd hear often from that crowd. To them, first-generation Italian kids weren't really Italian anymore. Just American.

I looked over at my dad as he finished preparing the bread-and-tomato lunch. He gave me a disappointed look, mostly because he knew Nick was right. As I got older, I did lose pieces of what made me Italian. At first, it was just learning to speak proper English; later, I drifted toward the American things that surrounded me. Eventually, I ran from being Italian altogether — something I regret now that I'm older and trying to reconnect with it.

Silently, my dad sliced a hunk of bread and tomato, wrapped it up, and handed it to me — a clear signal that I'd be walking home in the rain.

I grabbed my jacket, slid the car into my pocket, and sulked home, Charlie Brown style — head down, not caring if it was raining. My mom shouted something as I came in, but I didn't hear her. I went straight to my room, pulled the car out of my pocket, and stared at that black roof.

All I could hear in my head was Nick mocking me for being American.

I started picking at the black paint with my fingernail. It wouldn't budge — those Mattel guys didn't mess around. So I grabbed a quarter from my piggy bank and started rubbing.

I rubbed and rubbed until the entire roof was bare. Underneath the paint was red die-cast metal, just like the rest of the car — which, of course, should have been obvious. Now I had to hide it from my mom, or she'd never buy me another toy car. I felt stupid. Stupid American Danny.

Later, my dad came home and walked straight to me.

"No lissen to Nick. He's an asso," he said. My dad rarely swore in any language, but I assumed he meant asshole. He paused, studying me. I think he was proud I hadn't gotten mad. "Nicola's mad at everyone because his wife is a whore. So no worry about what he says."

I don't know if his wife really was a whore, but I do know they split up, and

Nick later married a young American woman who worked for a semiconductor company — and he never worked again.

Still, I'd defaced my car because he got under my skin. A lesson learned, I guess.

The car itself is perfect except for the roof. The wheels are straight, and it still rolls nicely.

As for me — maybe I'm a little smarter now. But I don't need the constant reminder of being taunted.

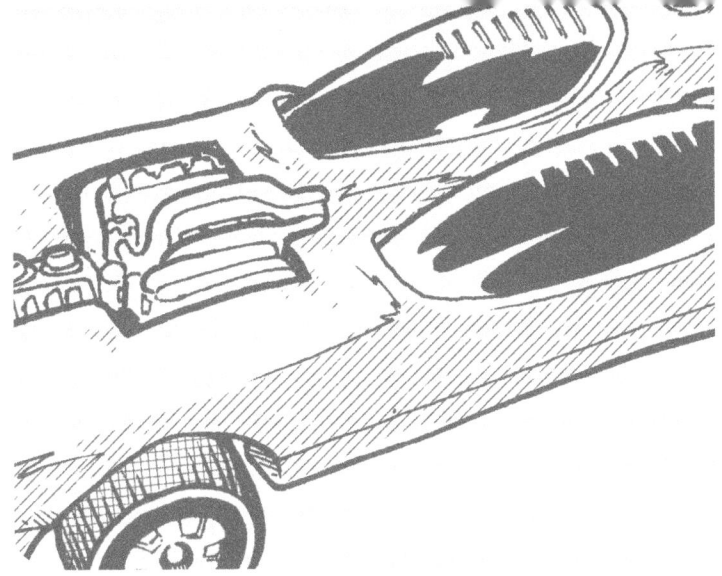

Splittin' Image
1968

If ever there was a car made to race, it was my beloved Splittin' Image. This car was heavy and sturdy, with nicks and chipped paint, yet it had the soul of a champion, almost never losing.

I did not realize it at the time, but the name is a play on words. The car has two separate cockpits, separated by a long exhaust pipe that runs from the oversized, exposed engine at the front of the car to the back, covering what would be the trunk area. Instead of a trunk, the car had two giant tanks to put gas.

Why would you separate the passengers like this? I have no idea. It seems unsafe and impractical to me, and who would want to have two passengers in a high-performance test vehicle, since the extra weight would only slow it down.

At any rate, this car was fast ,and it was quicker than other Splittin' Images that found their way to my house on Maywood Ave. Maybe I got a diamond in the rough, or maybe this was the universe's way of making up for my rough start in school.

Much like I had a favorite car, I had a favorite teacher. Mrs. Bruno. Yes, there is a vowel at the end of the name, but she married into it. I had her in second grade, and if it were not for her, the school principal would probably still be speaking to me in Spanish because he thought I was Mexican.

Mrs. Bruno understood the trouble I was having learning to read and how I was almost held back in the first grade. Stuff like that gets out, and pretty soon, all of your friends are thinking you are dumb. I wasn't dumb, I was just having a hard time with the English language. In first grade, my teacher told my mom to give me anything I wanted to read, no matter what it was. So, desperately wanting me to catch up to the other kids, my mom would take me to magazine racks and bookstores, point at the shelves, and say "Read something!", and I gravitated to Dr. Seuss books and comic books. The comics were for sure over my head, and even over the head of most first graders, but I loved the goofy Superman stuff and always thought I could one day be a stand-in for Superman's Pal Jimmy Olsen. This time in my life predated my Hot Wheels collecting by a couple of years.

I spent the summer between first and second grades devouring any comic book I could get my hands on and, since comics are a visual medium, I was able to piece together the meaning of some reasonably complex words.

Once fall hit I was reading a lot better, although I did not really realize how much better. I was still being given remedial-level stuff, and to be honest, I didn't really know my reading assignments were dumbed down, only that I seemed to be passing them more quickly. Mrs. Bruno noticed though, and often commended me "I guess a switch just flipped in your head" she would say, smiling at me. I liked it when Mrs. Bruno was happy and especially when she was delighted with me. Mrs. Bruno, beyond being sweet, was one of the most attractive teachers in my school. She didn't know about my reading comic books, only that I was doing better.

Flash forward a few weeks and it's now October. I am reading some Superman comics where he is battling Bizarro Superman. I loved this because of the way Bizzaro spoke and how everything good was bad and everything bad was good. But I didn't quite get why they were called Bizarro (I didn't have the origin story, just a mess of Superman or Action Comics that featured Bizarro). I wanted to find out what this word meant, so I jotted it down on a piece of paper and brought it to school the next day.

Just as we were letting out for lunch, I walked over to Mrs. Bruno, who was smiling as wide and bright as I had ever seen her smile, as she was going to lunch with Mr. Clayton, a teacher I would later have in fifth grade. He was a good-looking guy, too, and together he and Mrs. Bruno seemed like the king and queen of Moorpark Elementary. I ran up to her just as she was getting up to her desk, my paper clutched in my hand.

"Can you help me with a word, Missus Bruno?" I said as I placed the paper down on her desk. "I don't recognize it, but I see it a lot in the comic books I read."

Mrs. Bruno took the paper in hand and sounded out, "Biz-arr-o?" she said, sort of stumbling on the word and its pronunciation. "You saw this in a comic book?" By now, Mr Clayton had joined us and was interested in what was going on as he took the paper from Mrs. Bruno, smiling at her as he did.

"In a comic book, well my goodness, they use such interesting words in those things, don't they?" she said, smiling that smile that made me forget my name, "What was going on in this comic book?" she asked, hoping I would guess to get some context.

So I told her all about the Bizarro Superman and how he was the opposite of Superman, how the world he lived on was square, not round, that anything bad was good, and that conversely anything good was bad. Hate meant love, and everyone hated Superman the most.

Mrs. Bruno had an ah-ha moment, "Oh, I get it, Bizarro is a bizarre version of Superman. Bizarre - Bizarro."

Now the light came on in my eyes, and I interrupted just as Mrs. Bruno was about to explain the word bizarre to me, but I saved her the trouble by explaining it myself. "I get it. He's weird and strange, so he's a bizarre Superman...BI-ZARRO! THANKS MRS. BRUNO!" I yelled as I started to turn and run out to the yard for lunch.

"Wait, Danny..." I hated being called Danny, but I liked it when Mrs. Bruno did it because it sounded so warm and kind- I felt good inside; it was sweet-sounding and not at all mean. "...You know what the word bizarre means?" she asked.

"Uh, yeah," I said, hoping I wasn't in trouble.

"Well, doesn't that just take the cake then? What other words do you know?" It was about here that Mr. Clayton stepped in, gently tugging on Mrs. Bruno's arm, saying, "Lunch is almost over, Carla..."

"Oh yes, lunch," she said, a little flabbergasted, then she turned to me and said,

"We will talk later after school, ok?" That was both a question and a command. I liked hanging around Mrs. Bruno, so I didn't feel like I was being punished for something.

It would be a few years before I understood what the big deal was about knowing the word 'bizarre,' or any of the other words I learned from reading comics. Bizarre is a 4th-6th grade level word, you would not see it in second grade level materials, so for me to know it and use it in a sentence without thinking about it told Mrs. Bruno that my reading level was well above what they understood it to be. I started reading harder books, and I remember feeling alternately bored and challenged. Pretty soon, some of the other teachers were telling parents to let their kids read comics, which was cool until one day at lunch, my friend Michael decided he was Spider-Man and Bart was the Green Goblin, and the two of them proceeded to fight each other while hanging all over the jungle gym like it was The Empire State Building.
WHY IS THIS A "...COOL UNTIL..." MOMENT?

So, you ask, what, if anything, does this have to do with The Splittin' Image, since this happened a couple of years before Hot Wheels even existed? Well, I am glad you asked. Years roll by and now I am in fifth grade, and Mr Clayton is my teacher. He was in the habit of sending notes to Mrs. Bruno during class and somehow I wound up becoming the courier, I think, because they both trusted me enough not to read the note and just deliver it without question. Sometimes they would have entire conversations through these notes, with me running back and forth as I was instructed to wait for a reply.

One day Mr. Clayton went to the office during recess, and when he got back, he did not seem happy. I watched him reach for the notepad and start scribbling something, which was my cue to come to his desk and pick up the note. Mr Clayton sort of shoved it at me and demanded that I "Wait for a reply." Mr. Clayton's voice had an angry tone to it and it served to spoil what had been a pretty good recess. Some of the Sunday group had brought a couple of cars each from home and were playing with them in the dirt as we started making up stories for our cars. I had brought the Splittin' Image because if any car I owned was cool enough to write stories around, this one was it.

I took the note and walked to Mrs. Bruno's room. When I got there, I could see she was visibly upset. I stopped walking and considered leaving, but she looked up at me, smiled, and motioned for me to come over. As I got closer, I could see she was crying, right in front of her class, too. I had never encountered an adult crying, and Mrs. Bruno was having a silent sob, and it shook me up. I didn't know what to do, so I just held the note out.

Mrs. Bruno took the note from me, opened it, then tore it up and put it in her wastebasket. I started to turn away as Mrs. Bruno tried to compose herself. She was NOT doing a good job of it; if anything, she was getting even more upset. I shoved my hands in my pockets and started to leave when I noticed that one of my cars was still in there. I pulled out The Spittin' Image.

"Hey, Mrs. Bruno," I said as I held out the car. "This is my favorite car in my collection. It's super fast and it's heavy and tough. Would you like to keep it on your desk?"

Mrs. Bruno took the car from my hands and rolled it across the glass top of her desk, making it seem even faster than it was. She had stopped crying and was using a tissue to dry her eyes. "Thank you Danny," she said, regaining her composure.

"Not FOREVER though," I added quickly, "I will need it back before Sunday!"

Mrs. Bruno smiled and chuckled under her breath, saying, "Yes, of course. Thank You, Danny."

I got back to Mr. Clayton's room and went back to my desk. Mr Clayton gave me a look that was a cross between puzzlement and anger. He was, of course, waiting for a response. I just shrugged my shoulders at him and looked away, realizing right then that despite his being a good teacher, I did not much care for Mr. Clayton. At the end of the school year, Mr. Clayton was cleaning out his closets as he announced to the class that he would not be returning to Moorpark Elementary next year. He called me over to him on the last day of school and handed me a book.

"You're a smart kid, Danny, thanks for helping me with those notes." He reached into a box and pulled out a book; it was black and worn, like it had been well-read. "This is a little over your head right now, but keep it. Someday, you will understand." I looked down at the book's cover and sounded out the title.

"Mein Kampf"

I took the book home and put it on my desk, and didn't think about it. I am not sure how much time passed before I noticed it had disappeared. I was never going to read it anyway, so I did not much care.

Mrs. Bruno also told me that she was not coming back to teach either and that she was going to have a baby next fall, and she hoped I would not have too hard a time in sixth grade with Mr. Glenn.

I never found out what was in that note or what upset Mrs. Bruno so much, but I heard rumors when I got to middle school because the whole thing was scandalous. The most prevalent rumor was that Mr. Clayton and Mrs. Bruno were having an affair. My note running was helping them with their logistics. The reason Mrs. Bruno was so upset, though, was because on that day that I left the car on her desk, the husband of ANOTHER woman that Mr. Clayton was sleeping with came into the school to complain. Philanderer is a college-level word, and I heard it a lot when people talked about Mr. Clayton.

I did get my Splittin' Image back, and I raced the heck out of it that summer, leaving behind all the stress of being a courier for illicit messages during the school year.

Custom Barracuda
Part Two

First of all, yes — this is indeed the same Blue Custom Barracuda from the very first story, my very first car. I actually can't say with 100 percent certainty that this was the exact same car from the first story, but that's because it for sure was a car I felt I needed to have two of.

This car was one of my favorites for so many reasons: it was fast, cool, and everything I wasn't at the time. It was also a car I liked to show off now and then because it always got people talking. Of course, that wasn't always a good thing.

My friend Petra — who I was trying to get into our Sunday Maywood Avenue Post-Church (but not limited to Catholics) Invitational and Hot Dog Roast — had an older sister named Angela. Angela occasionally wound up at our house for pizza and snacks. She didn't like Hot Wheels. She didn't care about cars. But there she was, for the free pizza and the opportunity to make sure everyone knew that she was in high school and had SO MUCH STUDYING TO DO!

And Angela had was a boyfriend — a muscle-bound idiot named Rick who lettered in football, baseball, and picking on little kids. I was pretty young and had no reason to be around a guy like Rick, but somehow he always managed to find his way into my orbit, and every time he did, he picked on me and whoever I happened to be hanging out with — including Petra.

At least he did until this particular Sunday.

It was right after church, and I had brought a couple of cars to show Petra on the walk home (we were still not allowed to hang out outside of school because of the incident with the Beach Bomb surfboards). One of those cars was this very same Blue Custom Barracuda — a beauty of a machine, in my opinion.

Petra's love of cars came from her dad, a neighborhood mechanic who worked on everyone's vehicles. The man knew his stuff, and he passed that passion and knowledge down to his youngest daughter. Petra's dad was far less of a hard case about me than her mom, but holy cow, did he not like Angela's boyfriend!

So, after Mass, I was in the parking lot showing Petra the Barracuda when — out of nowhere — Rick appeared. He started shouting about the car.

"My uncle owns a REAL Barracuda that's almost the same color!"

He came in close, his hands in a kind of shrugging gesture, but I noticed one hand held out toward me, palm up — like he expected me to hand him the car.

"He'd really LOVE to have a toy like that..."

His voice trailed off, getting lower and more menacing. Rick fully expected me to give him the car.

I looked around for my mom, but she hadn't come for me yet (for reasons I didn't understand at the time, I had to go to church, but my parents didn't). Only Petra was there, but she was willing to intervene.

"LEAVE HIM ALONE, RICK!" she shouted.

The word "Rick" had barely left her mouth when her dad appeared — seemingly out of nowhere. He stood behind me, smiling like a tiger about to pounce on its prey.

"Son..." he began.

What followed was a string of obscenities so intense that, when strung together, they formed the filthiest sentence my young ears had ever heard —

ending with, "...and leave this kid alone."

This floored me because Petra's dad was a Mormon. He didn't smoke, he didn't drink, and he most certainly didn't swear. The strongest language I'd ever heard from him was "gosh-durn." But like any father with daughters, he was protective — and Rick had a way of bringing out the worst in people.

eBay would never let me write what he said here, but if you send me a message, I'll tell you. By today's standards, it was probably pretty mild, but to me, it was the most forceful stream of dirty words I'd ever heard in English. The color drained from Rick's face. Something told me this wasn't the first time he'd been chewed out like that. He pulled his hand back, slunk away, and never bothered me again.

As for the car — the wheels never really spun right, and while the paint looked shiny and blue when I first got it, the years haven't been kind. The color's faded a bit — much like Rick's pride that day after Petra's dad was done with him.

Bubble Gunner
1978

The Bubble Gunner came to me after the end of my Hot Wheels racing career. By that time, I had a real car — a '62 Buick Electra, which I'm sure was a badass in its day — a job making almost three dollars an hour, and nearly zero interest in spending my hard-earned "wealth" on a car I couldn't take a girl to the movies in.

But these cars had a way of finding their way to me, usually as gifts from people who'd say, "Do you still like Hot Wheels?" To which the answer was, of course, I still liked them. Liking them wasn't the issue. I had just turned seventeen and I simply found myself liking Jeanine in my algebra class a whole lot more than I liked Hot Wheels.

Jeanine,was amazing in just about every way, and she had to have pizza every Friday night before we hung out, or it was over for me. And if you had seen Jeanine, you'd understand — you'd make that trade any day of the week. She was like a teenage Farrah Fawcett. If there had been a poster of Jeanine, I'd have hung it on my wall in a heartbeat.

For context — since some of you may not know who she was — Farrah Fawcett was a TV and movie star whose major claim to fame was being one of the original Charlie's Angels. Fawcett was talented, beautiful, smart, and knew exactly how to market herself. Before Charlie's Angels, she became a pop-culture phenomenon thanks to a poster that featured her in a one-piece red bathing suit with her signature feathered hair — a look that every girl tried to copy. The poster became, and still remains, the best-selling poster of all time.

Fun fact: Farrah picked out the bathing suit herself, did her own hair and makeup, and even chose the final image for the poster. So when I compare Jeanine to Farrah Fawcett, I do not do so lightly — Jeanine had all of those same qualities.

So what does that have to do with the Bubble Gunner?

Well, the car — a green Blackwall (no Redline? come on!) — had a chrome engine and a green dome. Having been given the car, I naturally had to see what it could do. But alas, my old orange track had fallen victim to my mom's new obsession with having less of "da crap" in the living room.

Still, I decided to test it on the smooth hardwood floor where the track once ran.

Pulling the Bubble Gunner from its package, I placed it on the floor and gave it a gentle push forward. The car glided gracefully across the living room, coming to a stop somewhere near my mom's crochet pile. It moved beautifully — smooth wheel rotation, steady glide, almost as if it were self-propelled. Not fast, mind you, but elegant.

My expert professional opinion: it was too bulky to really achieve top speed on a proper track. If I'd brought it out during the old Sunday Speed Trials at my house, I'd probably have been laughed at. Kids were cruel — but if it had put in a decent performance, they would've stopped laughing pretty quick. I was quickly slinking back into a kid's mindset; the only real test was if I put this thing on some track, I know I had track somewhere. I could set it up and give her a trial, along with the other cars people gave me when I got to high school.

Then I realized that Jeanine was waiting, and the track would always be here and I had pizza and popcorn to buy. So off I went to pick Jeanine up in my non-hotwheels equivelant car. It was the right thing to do.

Realizing this, I decided that choosing Jeanine over Hot Wheels was something that turned me into an adult.

Well, not really, but it contributed.

Purple Funny Money
1970

Controversy swirled around our house when this car came into our family. I had an uncle, a nice man and an air force veteran, who was not down with the hippie imagery on the side of the car. Peace signs, yellow happy faces and sunshine had cost us the war in Viet Nam.

My mom, an immigrant who had lived through a war in Europe would say "What's your problem with peace?" to which my uncle had pretty much no response. He did not understand that my mom, who herself had fascist tendencies having grown up under one, was asking sincere questions and not trying to be a mean.

"You have to be STRONG to make peace" he would say "Hippies are KILLING this country, all flowers and love and pot smoking and crap." My mom would tell me to leave the room when he got on one of these tirades because he would always land on hippies and smoking pot, and she did not want me to be exposed to notions of either. My uncle though would chase me down to continue the conversation.

"Kid, do you think smiley faces and hippy flowers are going to end the war? THEY WILL NOT!" he shouted to me on more than one occasion. "We dropped a BOMB on Japan, then we had peace real quick!"

This was a common sentiment at the time, that the notion of wanting peace was somehow hindering us from achieving it. The idea that maybe we, as a country, did not have to fight in every war and that assigning a won/loss record to conflicts was not a healthy way of determining the strength of a country or society. I had just discovered John Lennon's "Give Peace a Chance" even though that song came out in 1969.

My parents did not want me listening to the Beatles because they were all smoking marijuana and using drugs and this song, in particular, enraged the adults in my life. Maybe the song and the sentiment inspired the car; I have no idea. All I knew was I would hear people get all pissed off about it, and the people from The Greatest Generation seemed most offended by it. When I heard the song I asked my dad why people were so angry about the song and about my car and about all things that seemed sort of nice to me as a 10 year old.

"The song just says 'Give Peace A Chance', what's so bad about that?" I asked.

"That guy smokes too much marijuana" My dad replied, never really addressing my question.

At any rate, I listed this car as used due to its age and because it is not in the original package. However It was not used at all as I hid it out of deference to the uptight squares who were often in my presence and always had something to say about anything I was doing.

And to be honest this did not look like a car that would pass race muster, as all I cared about was speed anyway.

I didn't even get to my confusion about the name of the car, because it seemed so out of place, but that's maybe a different story.

Beach Bomb
1969

The defining feature of this die-cast toy was the same thing that kept the price down when I tried to sell it: the missing surfboard.

Many cars from that time had removable parts, and over the years those parts were often lost to the winds of time. If you asked the current owners what happened to them, you'd probably just get a shrug and an "I dunno…" in response.

But I remember all too well what happened to the surfboard—and it all has to do with my friend Petra. Or more specifically, Petra's mom.

As a way of making the Maywood Avenue Hot Wheels Racers and Pizza Aficionados group more inclusive, Petra's mom offered to host a Sunday afternoon gathering. My parents—still hopeful for another child or maybe just wanting some alone time—quickly agreed and sent me over with all my track, cars, and accessories for an afternoon of hot dogs and pink cupcakes.

Being a champion of letting the girls race (except maybe for that one neighbor's cousin who had no interest in anything other than being disruptive and refusing to eat the crust of her pizza), I had no problem with it. Besides, I had overheard my parents engaged in post-church hosannas one too many times and could use a break. I knew there'd still be Sunday dinner waiting for me at home, so the subpar food (by my standards) was something I could tolerate.

At any rate, Petra's mom had put out a spread of assorted snacks (nothing healthy) and sodas. There was also a tray of cold cuts for the few adults present—a polite gesture, but one that didn't impress me. I'm Italian, and my average school lunch could put most modern charcuterie boards to shame. Still, my mother raised a polite boy, so I simply ignored the tray, confident there'd be something better waiting for me later.

I should have paid more attention, though. When I glanced over at the tray—just in case there was a cracker I might find acceptable—I was horrified to see that Petra's mom had taken my Beach Bomb from my tray of cars and placed it in the cold-cut dish!

Not directly in the food, but right alongside it. And that wasn't even the worst part. She had removed the surfboards and used them to decorate slices of pineapple on the adult platter!

That was it for me. I gathered my cars and went home on the spot. But in my haste, I left the surfboards behind. When I went back, I could only find one—and Petra's mom, who had already decided I was an insolent brat and had called my mom to tell her so, was no help at all.

So, here are your takeaways:

First, this car did not touch food. It was used as decoration only. Petra's mom may have been misguided, but she wasn't gross—she would never have placed a dirty toy of unknown origin on or in any food. So bid with confidence: there is absolutely no trace of poorly cured salami or Oscar Mayer bologna on this car.

Second, though it took me a while to stop blaming Petra, this incident taught me to judge everyone on their own merits and not hold them responsible for someone else's actions.

Lastly, if you're an adult who needs "quiet time" away from your kids, wait until they've gone to bed. Otherwise, you risk being interrupted by someone like Petra's mom—who will be eager to tell you what a brat your kid is.

Maserati Mistral
1969

There were a lot of Italian cars that populated the Hot Wheels Redline series back in the mid-to-late '60s — or maybe it just seemed that way because any car with a vowel at the end of its name caught my eye, and more specifically, my dad's.

My father was very proud of his heritage. While he didn't wear it on his sleeve like some people, he made no bones about the fact that he was an Italian living in America — not Italian-American. There's a distinction there, and it's not as subtle as you might think. For example: if you go to a restaurant and they serve "spaghetti and meatballs," that's Italian-American. In Italy, pasta is its own thing — you rarely serve it with something else, and never as a side dish.

One of the founding principles of Sunday dinner — where pasta was always served first — was that when you were called to the table, you sat down, drank your wine, and continued whatever conversation you were having until a plate of pasta was put in front of you. Our current polite society says you wait until everyone is served before you start eating, but in an Italian household, when the pasta hits the table, you start eating. That's how it's meant to be enjoyed: hot and fresh. You don't gulp it down like a savage, but you don't wait either.

Once everyone was done, the leftover sauce on the plate had to be mopped up with bread — a ritual called "fare la scarpetta." For me, being stuck between two languages, that was confusing, since scarpetta means "little shoe."

But this isn't a story about pasta. Honestly, it's barely a story about cars. It's really a story about times — and how things change — and about something that happened, that could never (or at least should never) happen again.

It was the middle of the week at Moorpark Elementary School, which meant we'd all gotten our fill of shocking each other by rubbing our feet on the newly installed carpet in class. A freeway was being completed just above the school, so someone decided that our classrooms would get carpeting to deaden the sound — and air conditioning so we wouldn't need to open the windows and breathe in exhaust fumes. Luxurious indeed. It almost made me want to go to school. Almost.

The district had installed the carpet over winter break, and brand-new commercial carpet in those days was basically an electric generator: rub your feet on it fast enough and touch someone — zap! It was funny for a while, but soon, after getting shocked yourself a few too many times, it got old.

During one of these post-zapping lulls, as class was starting, I was telling my friends about the Mistral my mom had just bought me and how I couldn't wait to try it out on the track that Sunday. I must've lost track of time or not heard the bell, because my teacher — a hateful man named Mr. Glenn — interrupted me to get me to quiet down.

"What's so important, Danny?"

This man is one of the many reasons I hate being called Danny. Sometimes he'd call me "Danny Boy," like in the song "O' Danny Boy", which, strangely, didn't bother me — it seemed somewhat affectionate. (In case you hadn't guessed, Mr. Glenn was Irish.)

"Uh, just talking about my new Hot Wheels car, Mr. Glenn. It's a Maserati!" I said, hoping I wasn't about to be made to stand in the corner during the Pledge of Allegiance again for interrupting class.

"Maserati, huh?" he said, with a look of realization crossing his face. "Italian car. Figures. Hey, Danny — have you heard about the new Italian snow tire?"

I was confused. Why would I have heard about snow tires? My only interest in cars was the die-cast kind I raced on Sundays, and those were mostly made in Hong Kong. Still, I decided to play along — I'd had my fill of standing in corners that year.

"Uh... no, I haven't," I said, hoping that would end it.

"Amazing tires!" Mr. Glenn declared, now in what we'd call "performance mode," as he walked toward me.

"DAGO TRU RAIN! DAGO TRU SNOW! DAGO TRU MUD! BUT WHEN DEY GO FLAT — DAGO WOP WOP WOP WOP WOP!" he shouted.

Let that sink in for a moment: this was a racist joke being told at my expense.

In school.

In front of the class.

By a teacher.

Mr. Glenn erupted in laughter. That wasn't surprising. What was surprising was the laughter coming from my classmates — including the other Italian kids. Most of them were second or third generation, Italian in name only. I was the only one who could actually speak Italian and had been to my parents' homeland several times — including once when I was still in diapers.

I was mad. No, I was beyond mad. I was enraged — "kick someone in the shins or set your cat on fire" mad. I wanted to cry, to yell, to call Mr. Glenn whatever Irish slur I could think of and tell him what a bully he was.

But then I closed my eyes and saw my dad through the blur of tears. In a very Obi-Wan kind of way, I remembered something he'd told me at the start of the school year, when he learned who my teacher was.

"He gonna try and make you mad," my dad had said. (In my mind, he's drinking a glass of wine with peaches in it — his thing — though that might just be a fond memory layered over the truth.)

"No get mad. That's what he want — for you to be mad and yell and get in trouble," he said, in the strong voice of his younger days. (Later, he'd be weakened by adult-onset muscular dystrophy, and I'd watch him wither into a shadow of himself. As I write this, I'm a year younger than he was when he died. The strong voice is the one I remember.)

"No give people wha' dey want," he said. "Make dem wonder wha' you thinking. Just smile and let God take care of dem."

I opened my eyes on those last words and pictured Mr. Glenn being eaten alive by worms, like King Herod — one of the few Bible stories that stuck with me.

So I didn't cry. I didn't yell. I just nodded, smiled, and let him laugh his ignorant little laugh. Then I looked around at the kids who'd joined in and made a mental note of who wasn't getting invited to the Maywood Raceway on Sunday.

Which brings me back to the Maserati Mistral Redline car.

My dad saw it in my collection and let out a whistle. "Mistral — very sporty looking," he said. Maserati bounced between being a racing brand and a luxury brand, and this model could be considered both.

"One day, I buy dat car and we gonna drive all over," he said. The Mistral was a two-seater, so I figured he planned on leaving my mom at home — a theme that would become more common as the years went by.

That afternoon, I burst into the house, went straight to my new car, and ripped it out of the package — I was going to race it. My mom saw me angrily setting up the track in the living room and asked what was going on.

"Mr. Glenn," I muttered.

That was all she needed to hear. A few minutes later, she brought me two Oreo cookies — her way of giving me an emotional pick-me-up.

I set up the track at dining-room-table height so the car would hit the straightaway with plenty of speed. But to my amazement, it didn't shoot down the track. It crawled down the slope and stopped short before the end. I tried again — same thing.

It looked amazing, but as a racer, it was a total dud. The wheels turned fine, but it just didn't move. So it ended up sitting at the bottom of my Redline Collector's Case — alone and unloved. Odd for a Maserati, since I'd kill to drive one now.

As for Mr. Glenn — I'm sure the worms have gotten him by now. I take comfort in that.

Custom Camaro
1967

This car — a 1967 Camaro in orange — holds a special meaning for me. Not because of its racing ability (it was average on my track on Maywood Avenue — not a winner, not a loser, just not fast enough to drag out every Sunday), but because, as with any good story, there are layers to my ownership of this Redline Hot Wheels car.

If this story is about any car, it's really about the first real car I ever owned: a 1961 Buick Electra that my dad bought for me when I got my license. I've mentioned the Buick before as being something of a piece of junk, and in some ways, it was. But in other ways, it was glorious — my pathway to freedom, adulthood, and so much more. I didn't realize it at the time, but the Buick became such an important car in my life that to this day, I can still see it parked in front of my old house on Maywood Avenue.

But, of course, I digress.

The titular Camaro in this story matters too — because it was a cool car that cool people drove, and I was still hoping that someday I'd be cool. It was also the model my high school used for Driver's Ed.

For the uninitiated, back in the 1970s, driver's education in California high schools included both Driver's Education (the classroom part, which still exists today) and Driver's Training the terrifying, behind-the-wheel, in-real-traffic part.

At Del Mar High, driver's training was taught by the football and PE coaches — all men, all capable of slamming their foot down on the passenger-side emergency brake while screaming at you until you learned to use your blinker. The car my school used was a Camaro, and it felt like fate. My 1967 orange Redline Camaro still sat on my desk at home, and I thought this had to be a sign. Learning to drive in a Camaro surely meant I was destined to drive one in real life — to finally be cool and leave behind my comic-book-reading, broken-English-speaking days forever.

As I got closer to finishing Driver's Training and getting my permit, my dad began asking what kind of car I wanted.

"A Camaro," I'd say, every time. "We drive one at school, so it only makes sense, right?"

His answer was always the same: silence and a puzzled look. That happened a lot between us in those days — not just about cars but about almost everything. Still, I tried to negotiate.

"I don't mean a new car — a used one would be fine."

Or, pointing at the one on my desk: "Wouldn't you like to go Sunday shirt shopping in this?"

Sunday shirt shopping was a ritual for us. After I got my license, every Sunday between church and dinner, my dad would tell me he wanted to "go buy a shirt." I'd drive him from store to store, sometimes for hours, until it was time to head home. In all those Sunday outings, I think he bought maybe two shirts.

Anyway — the day finally came when my dad summoned me and said, "Come on, we gonna get you a car." He handed me the keys to his station wagon and gave my mom a blank, cold stare — the kind that said an argument had just ended and she'd lost. I guess my getting a car that day was his way of proving who was boss.

I jumped up, shoved my feet into my shoes, and was out the door in record time! Behind the wheel, I asked where we were going. My dad said to drive to the end of the street, turn right onto Bascom Avenue, and keep going until we got to Los Gatos — a ritzy little town with an auto row full of high-end cars. We pulled into a Cadillac dealership.

Cadillac. My mind raced. Were we really going car shopping HERE? Was my dad about to buy his only son a Caddy? Would I be the slickest kid at Del Mar, pulling up to school in a brand-new Cadillac even though I lived five blocks away? Forget the Camaro — this was next level.

A salesman came out to greet my dad, all smiles — the same fake, overly polite smile I'd seen Americans give him before.

"Arnie," the man said, using the nickname my dad hated but never corrected. "Good to see you! Thanks for the help with the TV. Come on — the used cars are this way."

Ah. Of course. Used cars. That made sense. My dad wasn't about to buy me a new one, but maybe a used Camaro was in the cards — maybe even a '67. (This was 1975, so that wouldn't have been too old.)

We walked past the shiny cars on the lot, past a very cool Camaro that made my heart jump and then plummet when we didn't stop. We went right by the service department and into the back lot — where old, beat-up cars waited for attention. And there it was: sitting all by itself: Brown. Dented. Unloved — my first car.

A 1961 Buick Electra.

This was not a Caddy. It was not a Camaro. It wasn't a car I'd ever imagined driving. And it didn't have a Hot Wheels equivalent, so why would I ever want it? There were better cars on either side of it, and my brain struggled to process the idea that this was the car. It had a giant dent on the passenger side rear quarter panel and a color that could best be described as "pre-rusted." But when I looked inside, the interior was immaculate.

The salesman — let's call him Bill, because all my dad's American friends seemed to be named Bill — came up behind me.

"I know this sounds like a salesman's line," he said, "but this car was literally owned by a little old lady who only drove it to church and the grocery store. At $300, it's a steal."

I opened the door and climbed in. Power windows. Power seats. A back seat big enough to house a family of five.

Bill smirked. "Checking out the back seat, eh? I know how you kids think."

I didn't get the joke.

And I didn't like him. I'd seen Bill at my dad's TV shop before; my aunt Elsa insisted on a new Cadillac every other year, so my dad fixed Bill's TVs for free, and Bill helped keep my aunt in her precious Caddies.

Bill leaned over the car. "The engine's clean too — you should check it out."

I didn't know much about engines beyond oil changes. They'd covered the basics in Driver's Ed, but I'd been too busy thinking about Superman and girls to absorb any of it. Still, I couldn't let Bill know that. So I popped the hood — and that's when things went south.

Back in those days, hoods were held up by two heavy-duty springs, not the hydraulic arms cars use now. I lifted it above my head, and the springs immediately snapped. The hood came crashing down — fast enough to have taken my head off. I caught it mid-fall and yelled, "What the FUCK!"

That got my dad's attention. He didn't swear in any language and didn't tolerate it from me. But seeing me holding the hood, he turned to Bill and barked, "What kind of junk you tryin' to sell me?"

For a moment, my faith in my dad was restored. He wasn't about to be bamboozled.

Bill stared at the broken springs. "I can fix that," he said, running into the repair shop. I figured he was fetching a mechanic. Nope. He came back holding a broom handle. "Here, this should do it." He wedged it under the hood like a prop stick.

The engine compartment was massive — just a block of metal with eight cylinders. No electronics, no computers, no safety features, no nothing. Just raw mechanics.

"That solves that," Bill said.

My dad wasn't having it. "Whassa goin' on here? I'm not give you three hundred dollars for this!"

Bill looked at my dad, then at me. "How about a hundred?"

My dad stuck out his hand. "Sold."

My heart broke. As the keys to my first car changed hands, I realized I'd been hosed. This wasn't a Camaro. This wasn't even close. I was never going to hear the end of it from my friends.

But still — I drove it home. I was disappointed, sure, but I was driving my very own car. I could go anywhere I wanted. Gas was fifty cents a gallon (about three bucks in today's money). With a 20-gallon tank and nine miles per gallon, I could go to Big Sur and back on a single tank.

Not that I did. I sulked instead. I parked out front, went inside, and sat at my desk. The 1967 Hot Wheels Camaro stared back at me, taunting me, as the Buick loomed through the front window.

If this story ended there, it would just be another sad tale of an immigrant kid not getting what he wanted because his parents didn't understand modern America. But that's not where it ends — because of two things that made the 1961 Buick Electra awesome in every way that mattered to a kid driving his first car.

First of all, it was huge — 19.5 feet long. (For comparison, my current Toyota Highlander is just under 16.) It had power steering, a cavernous back seat, and a vacuum-tube radio that could pick up stations from half a state away. On Sunday nights, I'd drive to an open field, tune the radio just right, and listen to Wolfman Jack or The King Biscuit Flower Hour. I made every kind of memory a sixteen-year-old could with that car. It wasn't stylish by any stretch, but it was mine.

And secondly, it taught me that sometimes you just have to appreciate the things that come your way — because sometimes, they work out exactly the way they're supposed to.

I was actually sad the day my dad took me back to that same Cadillac dealership and bought me a brand-new car — something he thought was more appropriate for our fancy Sunday shirt-buying excursions.

The Redline Camaro eventually went into my stash of Hot Wheels cars, where it later rewarded me by selling for $330 — ironically, more than three times what my dad paid for the Buick.

The Camaro and the Buick always come to mind whenever I buy a car. And I still think: if I ever get the chance to own a Buick Electra again, I'll take it.

And Mattel — if you're listening — you really should make a Redline Hot Wheels version of the 1961 Buick Electra. That car deserves it.

Olds 442
1969

This is a 1969 U.S. Hot Wheels Redline Olds 442 with the original spoiler and white interior. Ignored by me during my youth, this car rarely raced because, despite occasionally being used as a cop car, I never really saw it as a racer. That's probably why it's still in such great shape. The wheels roll smoothly, and the car glides in a straight, satisfying line.

To be honest, I was never much of an Oldsmobile guy. My dad was a Chevy man, and my aunt drove Cadillacs — both brands that your average Italian immigrant might gravitate toward, depending on what they wanted out of life: Chevy for getting things done, Cadillac for showing off a little status.

My dad being a TV repairman, wanted something practical that could get him to and from service calls. (Back then, TVs were giant wooden furniture pieces that required two people to lift.) He wasn't one for flash. My aunt, on the other hand, was a cleaning woman at The Emporium — a department store of the time — and I could never figure out how she could afford a Cadillac and all her other useless nonsense on a cleaning woman's salary, all while owning a home and taking care of my grandmother.

Then I found out why. My father had been supporting both her and my grandmother — buying them a house and covering expenses — which meant my aunt could afford the Caddy because she was living rent-free.

And that fact lived rent-free in my mom's head. She hated both my aunt and grandmother beyond reason — and that hatred lasted until dementia set in and wiped away her grudges right along with her memory of me being her son.

But I digress.

On our block, there was one family who actually owned an Oldsmobile. I don't remember the model, but I do remember the guy who drove it. Every Sunday afternoon, he'd show up looking for my dad and say, "Hey, Arnie! You gotta see the new Olds!" — then burst into hysterical laughter.

After that, he'd always add, "Hey, can you come by and take a look at my TV?"

My father — an immigrant who didn't fully grasp the joke — would just nod politely. To be honest, it wasn't funny, especially when you hear it every weekend.

I never did see the guy's car, which was fine by me. And as far as I know, my dad never "popped by" to look at his TV — because in neighborhood code, "look at my TV" really meant "fix it for free, Arnie."

1937 Bugatti
1977

The Bugatti came into my life much later, when I was in my twenties. It was a gift — this time from a woman (a girl who was mostly a woman, if you know what I mean) who knew that I had once raced and loved Hot Wheels cars and thought she could curry favor with me by giving me this one.

I suspected the gesture wasn't entirely sincere — probably just the only car on sale at the Gemco where she worked — and that she hadn't put as much effort into finding me the "perfect" car as she claimed.

For one thing, the tires were blackwalls, not Redlines, which automatically made it inferior. Mattel had phased out Redline tires in 1977 — the same year I graduated high school — effectively marking the end of any romantic notion of childhood I had left.

Secondly, the Bugatti itself had a mixed pedigree. The young woman gave it to me as a symbol of my Italian heritage, which at that point was fading in importance as I tried to distance myself from my parents — as all good spoiled brats do right before they turn twenty-one.

The thing is, while the name Bugatti is indeed Italian — the company's founder, Ettore Bugatti, was born in Italy — it's not exactly an Italian car brand. Bugatti moved to Germany to start his company and later became a French citizen when he relocated the business to France.

My dad, in all his Napolitan ways, sneered when he looked at the little car and said, "No eh Italiano." He also sneered at the girl, though for entirely different reasons — which, if I'm being honest, was probably why I dated her in the first place.

I should have been more appreciative, but I couldn't hide my disdain for the car. I told her it was the kind of thing I'd never have raced on my Maywood Avenue track when I was a kid — serious racers only ran Redlines. She broke up with me soon after — not because of the car, but because I was, frankly, a jerk to her.

I regret that now. Not because I wish I still had the relationship, but because in the process of figuring out how to be a decent human being, I inadvertently scratched the paint off a few people. Losing that friend because of my own arrogance — and keeping the car as a reminder — became a small but meaningful building block in becoming a more complete person.

For the sake of completeness: the Bugatti company folded in the 1960s but was revived as an actual Italian car company in the late 1980s. I suppose that proves that if you wait long enough, everything finds its way home — whether it's a car, a girl, or a die-cast nerd like me.

Custom Mustang
1968

Do you remember your first love? The one where lightning came down from the heavens, struck you, and you knew — absolutely knew — that the person sitting across from you was going to be the one? The person who would be with you forever, the center of your universe, the reason you couldn't breathe if they didn't talk to you every day and tell you they loved you?

I've had several of those kinds of loves. They've come in and out of my life from every direction — invading my brain at night so I couldn't sleep, stirring feelings in my young body that had never been stirred before.

There's been a long list of "forever loves" in my life — girls I met in high school, girls I met at the amusement park where I worked, girls I met just about anywhere — until I finally met the one who actually was the one. After that, there were no more.

But this story is about the first. At least, I think she was the first. The first girl to capture my imagination so completely that I couldn't eat, couldn't sleep, couldn't function until I knew she was mine and only mine — forever and ever, until the next one came along.

I'm talking, of course, about Petra.

Petra Goodway. She of the missing surfboard on my Beach Bomb. She of the mechanic father. She who had her own Hot Wheels club (because she was probably one of the earliest examples of a feminist I'd ever encountered). She with the golden hair, the girl-next-door smile, and the green eyes that saw straight into my elementary-school soul. She who could make the sun shine brighter and the rain fall softly around us whenever she was near.

Petra.

She was the one — the first one who made the world make sense. Petra, who liked Hot Wheels, maybe not as much as I did, but enough to show up when it counted on Sunday afternoons. Petra, who smelled how I imagined the Garden of Eden must have smelled like: fresh, new, with roses and freshly cut grass (without triggering my allergies.)

Petra.

I'd met two kinds of Italian men: the creative, soulful romantics who'd lie on their backs for years painting ceilings, and the everyday Italians who'd lie on their backs watching soccer (calcio, to be specific) while drinking wine and complaining about their wives.

I saw myself as the first kind — the romantic. The one whose words could make women swoon (in theory anyway) and grown men cry, inspiring people to write books and poems about me. Petra, who wasn't Italian, had a smile that stirred my, then-unstirred, loins.

Fourth-grade Me thought Petra was the most beautiful girl in the world — maybe ever — and that she would, of course, be my forever love. Our lives together would be an endless stream of Sunday afternoons filled with pizza, Hot Wheels races, and laughing at our parents.

I was young, foolish, romantic — and maybe a bit of a weirdo, because who thinks about forever love in the fourth grade when you've only recently stopped having nap time?

But I decided to get an early start. I needed to show her how much I cared — to make a grand, dramatic gesture before my nemesis, Bart, made his move.

Bart was a good-looking kid, and his name alone made him cooler than me. His last name ended in a vowel, meaning he was part of my tribe, and he had piercing green eyes that probably melted hearts and made girls weak.

Which meant I needed something special — something meaningful. And there was only one possible gift: a brand-new Hot Wheels car. Not just any car, but a Custom Mustang — the car we'd one day have our forever adventures in.

I've mentioned before that I had two of most of my cars — one to race, and one for what my mom called a "collectum item." (She meant collectible, but she always said "collectum," as in "you collect 'em.")

I had two Mustangs. My racer was already beat to hell, so I took the mint one — my collectum Mustang — and slipped it into my pocket. Then I wrote a note. I figured being mysterious and not signing it would be romantic, because Petra would instantly know it was from me.

"This will be the car we explore the world in," I wrote, ending it with hearts and Xs.

I slipped the note and the car into her desk after the first recess bell rang and went out to play dodgeball (or some other game involving a big red ball). I got hit in the face — hard — and my cheek was bright red when the bell rang to go back inside.

Petra was already in the classroom when I got there — and she was fuming. Mrs. Bruno stood over her desk, pointing at the car and note.

"Who is responsible for this?" she asked.

Petra spun around, red-faced and furious. "IT WAS HIM! IT HAD TO BE HIM!" she yelled, pointing at Bart.

Bart blinked. "Wha—?"

Petra unleashed on him: "You're always looking at me! I see you! Why are you giving me things I don't want? What does this even mean?"

Bart looked confused, but started piecing it together fast. "I didn't give you that..."

Mrs. Bruno, probably recalling Bart's tendency to stare at Petra and the other girls during P.E., asked, "If you didn't give it to her, then who did?"

"The creep who's always playing with Hot Wheels," Bart said, pointing directly at me in a perfect J'accuse! moment.

Everything clicked for Petra — all at once. The missing surfboard on the van, the other car I'd given her, the thing in the parking lot with her sister's boyfriend — all of it. Her face turned crimson with rage and embarrassment.

Then, instead of yelling more, she grabbed the car and hurled it at me. "TAKE YOUR CAR BACK, YOU CREEP!"

I didn't move. The Mustang zipped past my head. The red from the ball that had hit my cheek earlier now blended perfectly with the deep scarlet of my humiliation. I died a little inside — not because I was embarrassed (that had happened before, though not like this), but because the first person Petra thought of when she saw the car wasn't me.

It was Bart.

I slumped in my chair as the laughter filled the room. The car hit the wall behind me — the hood popped off. No matter how hard I looked, I couldn't find it.

Mrs. Bruno sent me to the principal's office, but nothing came of it. I went back to class and was told not to talk to Petra again.

I didn't care. I couldn't get over the fact that when Petra got that note, she thought it came from someone else.

I was sure no one would ever love me. Petra was the only person who might have understood me — and she thought someone else had written my love letter in die-cast metal.

I thought I'd never survive.

But, of course, I did.

And when that car resurfaced decades later, ready to be sold, all I could think of was Petra — my first love in the pure, ridiculous, fourth-grade way. I wondered if she and Bart ever ended up together.

If they did, I assume my invitation was lost in the mail.

Ferrari 312P
1969

This is a Hot Wheels Red Line Ferrari 312P in aqua — vintage 1969. It was one of the few cars my dad ever took an interest in — mostly because of him being an immigrant from Napoli, and he believed that almost anything ending in a vowel was automatically amazing.

In this case, he was right.

Even though it was just a die-cast toy, this vintage Ferrari moved like a Ferrari should — or at least how I imagined one would. Smooth, fast, never jumping the track, and winning more often than losing. When I'd pull out my cars, my dad would walk by and ask, "Ferrari?" To which I'd usually say, "No," preferring the heft and toughness of my beloved Silhouette.

My dad had a shrug that could start world wars — a quiet, subtle head motion that said he was annoyed with you and that whatever bad thing had happened, or about to happen, was not his fault, not his problem, and not his responsibility. It was always accompanied by a small utterance of the word "boh."

Boh is Italian slang for "I dunno," but it means much more than that. When my mom heard my dad say "Boh," dishes would start flying, and dinner was usually a silent affair — me sitting between two people who loved each other enough to murder one another and call it a crime of passion.

Anyway, I got the "boh" more often than not. But this was also around the time I started realizing that not everything was about me — and that maybe, just maybe, I wasn't racing the Ferrari because my dad loved it so much. Maybe I was rebelling for no reason. Maybe I cost myself a few good moments with him over a toy car.

Much, much later in life, while cleaning out my parents' house, I found a pile of old papers. Among my mom's endless collection of junk mail was a letter my dad had received from the Air Force.

When my dad immigrated to the United States, he joined the Air Force and served for several years, moving around the country until finally settling in the Bay Area, where he would later meet my mom, another Italian immigrant. At one point, he was stationed in New Mexico and used to claim he opened the first pizza restaurant in the state. He said he had to tell people the pizzas were "Italian tortillas."

My mom once told me that my dad joined the Air Force because he thought it would make becoming a U.S. citizen easier. It didn't. And reading that old Air Force letter surprised me — and made me a little sad.

In the letter, dated 1959 (the year I was born), my dad had tried to re-enlist and requested to be stationed in Italy. The reply was polite but firm: the Air Force assigned people where they were needed, not where they wanted to go. I imagine he could just as easily have been sent to Alaska. The letter ended with a line hoping he would "find a way to make a go of it in the U.S."

My dad eventually became a citizen in 1961, two years after I was born. I had never known him to struggle with life in America — by the time I was old enough to notice such things, he already seemed like the master of his own world.

So, in retrospect, it's no surprise that the Ferrari — this beautiful little red-line racer — brought a smile to his face. It constantly beat other cars of other makes on my orange track, and that small triumph must have meant something to him. It was a symbol of Italian pride, even though my dad always drove American (Chevys, mostly).

The irony, of course, is that the toy car was made in Hong Kong — so it was Italian only because we decided it was.

As for the car itself: it still rolls beautifully. The decals were never applied quite straight, but they're all there. The front shows just the right amount of wear for a champion. The hood opens, though not far enough to really show off the engine inside.

But then again — boh.

Silhouette
1971

This was my favorite car to race on the Sunday Maywood Avenue Post-Church Race Car Derby and Pizza Lunch Extravaganza track. I loved it enough to own three of them at one point. The other two were beaten like red-headed stepchildren and tossed aside once the wheels fell off from the abuse I heaped on them. But this one I rarely raced; it lived on my shelf of honor and then on my dresser—one of only two cars that followed me into high school and beyond my racing days, the other being the Camaro.

The Silhouette, based on a concept car of the same name, had a space-age look—part car, part spaceship. In my imaginary Hot Wheels world, the Silhouette would scream down the freeway, hit top speed, the exposed engine would spool up, and the entire car would lift off into orbit. The clear dome offered a near-360° view of the stars and the beautiful blue-and-white planet below. It was romantic in a way the other cars weren't because it promised adventures the others couldn't.

That's adult me talking. I was nine when I got this car, and my thought was simply: "Neat—a car and a spaceship!"

Also, it was fast. The blue one (the one I still had, and the one I was selling here) was among my fastest cars. Maybe not the fastest, but beautifully quick and stylish. That's adult me again, looking back at how it slid down that orange track. The kid in me just thought, "OOOOOO FAAAAASSST!"

This car became the vehicle that took me to my happy place—a spot I needed with increasing frequency as I got older, which is why it wound up on my dresser. If my mom yelled at me, I'd go to my room, run a hand over the sleek body, and find a little zen. If school gave me grief, the Silhouette reminded me that a fantastic future awaited. I fell in and out of love throughout high school, but through it all I could always imagine myself in the Silhouette's cockpit, rocketing into orbit for a quick visit to the stars.

The Silhouette was waiting on my dresser the last time I saw Petra. If you've read this far, you know who Petra is and what she meant to me. We didn't talk much after the car-throwing incident at school and the stern scolding I got from everyone. In retrospect, if that incident happened today, I'd probably have a file following me around as a potential stalker. I grew up in a boys-will-be-boys age, though, so once everyone had their two cents and believed I was sorry and wouldn't do anything that dumb again, they left me alone. I played with the Silhouette a lot then, masking my embarrassment with imaginary adventures in low-Earth orbit.

The distance between my desk and Petra's in our sixth-grade class was only a few feet, but as far as she was concerned I might as well have lived in a leper colony on the other side of the Grand Canyon. That year I swore off crushes; they were counterproductive. The world wasn't ready for a Custom-Car Casanova who spoke his love in poems written in die-cast metal. (That's adult me talking again. Sixth-grade me just thought, "Girls... I dunno.") The Sunday races were starting to wind down too. We no longer raced every week, and once my mom caught wind that kids were asking what was for lunch before coming over—"Dis no a restaurant! Dey eat what I give 'em—let dem eat McDonald!"—the end was near. It's natural for boys to age out of toys, only to become adults and spend paychecks buying them back at ridiculous prices on eBay, and was entering that age. The toys were the first to go; then the comic books. Middle school loomed; a Renaissance man like me would have no time to roll cars down plastic track.

Which brings us back to Petra. At year's end our school held a sixth-grade dance. No graduations then—just a farewell before we marched into middle school. I didn't want to go, but my mom made me. My parents had begun worrying tthat heir son was turning into a weirdo, and the Petra incident hadn't helped. Petra was the reason I didn't want to go, but my mom wanted me to learn how to act around girls, and my dad probably just wanted me out of the house for half an evening.

So off I went, dressed like a dork in a suit jacket, slacks, and the same dress shoes every kid wore to weddings and funerals. I refused a tie, which gave me the slightest whiff of cool. Once I arrived at the gym I beelined to the snack table, grabbed a soda, and then drifted to the perimeter to let the shadows swallow me like a grade-school ninja. That was the plan, anyway. Most of my friends were also in the shadows; the girls clustered on the other side. A couple brave souls danced in the middle—two girls together. I was years away from thinking that was hot; to me they were just grooving and giggling about whatever sixth-grade girls giggle about. Michael—the sixth-grader with the deep voice and facial hair—had wandered onto the stage to inspect the records. For all his faults, Michael had hip taste and could listen to whatever he wanted at home. Michael introduced me to the Beatles, a favor I never fully repaid.

I actually started to have fun. Michael had taken over spinning records from Mr. Glenn, and the room felt festive. I checked the clock—my mom would be back at 8:00 p.m., so I had half an hour to kill. Back at the snack table, I nearly swallowed my tongue: there stood Petra in a pink dress, looking every inch the girl next door. She saw me freeze and motioned me over.

"Hi," she said. Petra had a special "hi"—breathy and sweet, but not sexy (not that I could have processed that anyway), stretched into two syllables by a soft "h" and a wavering "iii". It meant she wanted your attention—and you gave it.

"Sorry I broke your Mustang. I shouldn't have thrown it at you," she said, a hint of remorse in her voice.

"Uh, it's okay. I shouldn't have done what I did—especially at school," I replied, swallowing the fact that I never found the hood. I'd brought it on myself, being overly romantic for a sixth-grader.

"Yeah, you shouldn't have," she said—warmly, not mean. "Why are you always trying to give me cars?"

A fair question; I had tried it more than once. If I were truly a romantic, I'd have had a Wonder-Years-style line ready. All I managed was, "Your dad's a mechanic, and you like cars—especially the fast ones."

"Especially the fast ones," she echoed, swaying so her dress seemed alive. She glanced over her shoulder at the floor, then back at me. "Do you want to dance?"

She might as well have asked me to skydive. Dance? Me? With PETRA? I didn't know how to dance fast, which is the music the school played to keep us from touching. My attempts looked like seizures—flailing arms and weird faces.

"Uh... no, I don't think so," I said, meekly.

"You wanted to drive me around the world in a Mustang with no hood, but you don't want to dance with me?" she snapped—accurately. This was a golden opportunity. For all my childish fantasies, this was why you stash the toys and try to make your voice sound deep at school.

"I mean, I don't know how..."

She looked at the dance floor again and back at me. "Neither do they," she said, and took my hand, leading me to the middle. Determined. Confident. I went along, hoping everyone would be looking at her. A Beatles tune was playing— Michael had clearly seized the turntable. Petra did a kind of modified twist, her dress spinning to the beat. I just shifted my weight side to side, added the occasional hop, and rolled my eyes toward heaven in hopes God would turn me into a dancer —at least for a few minutes. I thought people were probably laughing at me, so I just tried not to make eye contact with Petra because I knew I looked ridiculous.

The song ended. Another began—a slow one: "Sleep Walk." I glanced at Michael, now seated behind the turntable, flashing me a thumbs-up. Every Italian boy—probably every boy—has slow-danced with a dowager aunt at a wedding. I had, with my Zia Elsa, who always seemed to smell like mothballs and chicken soup. I reached for Petra to see if she wanted to keep dancing, and she did. I took her right hand with my left, placed my other hand in the safest place on her hip, and, arms fully extended, moved her slowly around the floor.

Mr. Glenn hustled over, shined a flashlight in my face, and growled, "That's as close as you get, hear me?" He didn't call me a name, but I'm sure he had one queued up.

I was not going to miss Mr. Glenn.

Petra and I synced up. I'd grown taller; she had to lift her chin to look at me. She looked sad. I glanced down to check I hadn't stepped on her foot (I did that to Zia Elsa once and I'm pretty sure that's why she cut me out of her will).

"I'm moving away," Petra said, sounding even sadder than she looked. "My parents are getting a divorce, and my dad is taking us to Utah."

For all my confusion at being between Italian and American, Petra maybe had it worse. Her dad was Mormon; her mom was raised Catholic. Love had bridged their differences—despite family objections, I'm sure—and they'd started a family. But then Petra's mom disappeared for a few months during the Summer of Love. Parents would whisper, and then stop when kids came near. She returned weeks later—seemingly the same outside, different inside. They kept up appearances, but it wore them down. Her mom stared north toward San Francisco in a half-daydream. Her dad grew gruff and bitter—"Hippies ate all the buffalo in Golden Gate Park," he'd say, or my favorite, "Pot smoking is a DISEASE!" Divorce wasn't common back then; knowing someone in one was like having a friend with cancer—impossible not to see as fatal.

"Moving away? To Utah?" I stammered, deploying my new superpower of stating the obvious. Petra didn't answer—she just lowered her head and closed the gap. Her head found a spot that would later be a sweet spot on me: top of her crown against my collar, her chin resting on my chest. Sixth-grade me grew up a little right then. It would be easy to sexualize the moment, but I understood: Petra didn't want to dance. Petra needed a hug. Mr. Glenn was busy trying to pry Michael from the records; and Michael, bless him, slipped on another slow song. He might have feared my mom, but he had zero fear of Mr. Glenn, and may have welcomed one more skirmish before middle school.

"Why?"

"I don't really know," she mumbled into my shirt. She did know. And she knew Utah would be rough with an angry, bitter single dad. We swayed. I searched for words to help, but came up empty. If I'd learned anything from being on the receiving end of my mom's shoe, it was that sometimes the best thing to say is nothing. So I said nothing.

A commotion drew eyes to the stage—Mr. Glenn was ready to drag Michael off by the collar. I caught Michael's eye and tried to send a "save yourself" look. He ignored me, then wisely climbed down on his own. Mr. Glenn slammed on a faster record to keep bodies apart.

Petra's smile faded. She went from looking at me to staring at her shoes. I was confused—still am—about why she'd come to me for comfort. We weren't close. Usually she rolled her eyes and left the room when I walked in. Did Petra like me... like that?

"Can I ask you something?" she said, locking eyes with me, not really waiting for permission. "What do you want?"

I didn't get it. I wanted lots of things: pizza every day, a new Hot Wheels every month, Star Trek not to be canceled. Right now I wanted to keep dancing with Petra and was devising schemes to keep her in California so we could be a special kind of friends as we grew up.

"You know—in life. What do you want?" she clarified.

No one had asked me that before. Adults always asked what we wanted to be when we grew up. Baseball player? Race-car driver? Anything but a TV man? I looked at Petra—sad, radiant, somehow prettier than when she walked in.

"I dunno... be happy, I guess."

That was it. All any of us want. I couldn't have known at eleven how heady and existential this was, now viewed through adult lenses. But there it was—the basis of life—summed up in the middle of my elementary school gym.

Petra stepped closer again—conspicuous, given the uptempo song. She rested her head on my chest and murmured into my shirt, "Yeah. Me too." Mr. Glenn targeted us, marching our way, but Mrs. Bruno intercepted, pointing to the rear exit with a concerned look. He pivoted and stormed off as Mrs. Bruno smiled seemingly satsfied. I think Mr.s Bruno generally liked messing with Mr Glenn, but then a part of felt she was giving Petra and I this moment, and the moment was beautiful and something that I think about to this day. I would've stayed like that, swaying with Petra to the sound of whatever music was playing until old age took us both, but the sight of my mom in the doorway made me break away.

"Uh... I have to go," I said clumsily.

"Yeah. I see," she said, looking past me. Not wanting my mom to see me hugging Petra, I stuck out my hand and shook hers.

"You can write me when you're in Utah," I said.

"Yeah. That's a good idea. I will," she replied. (She never did, but then I didn't either.) I turned toward my mom. Part of me wanted to run back and ask Petra to look for the surfboard from my Beach Bomb, but the dreamer in me decided that if she found it, she should keep it as a memento—a reminder of Sunday after church. I even imagined she'd made it into a necklace and would wear it on her wedding day as something old—a secret only she and I would understand. Doubtful.

I reached the door, doing my best not to meet my mom's eyes.

"Who dat girl?"

"Nobody, Mom."

"Wha' you mean nobody? She no look like nobody to me." I almost reminded her Petra had eaten lunch at our house, but I didn't need a deep dive on why I should only marry an Italian girl. We drove home in silence. After a quick hello to my dad, I went to my room and sat on the bed, trying to process the night—if not my entire life, all eleven years of it. "Let It Be" was still on my turntable (perk of being a TV man's son: the best audio gear, which at the time I didn't appreciate). I spun it up, volume low—professional equipment meant I could only crank it when no one else was home. Side Two was up. I let the guitar intro of "I've Got a Feeling" pull me to the edge of the bed. That album had practically lived on my turntable since I bought it with birthday money a year ago. The themes—loss, confusion, hope—resonated.

Yes, that's adult me talking. But it might've been kid me too. Either way, I loved that record. I sat cross-legged (what uptight parents called "Indian style"), trying to sort the night—and my life. On the dresser sat my Blue Silhouette with White Interior. A few years earlier I would've set up the track and rolled it around. Instead, I stood, stroked the cool die-cast curves, and thought about launching into orbit. I'd never looked closely at the interior beyond noting it was white. Tonight I peered in, imagined the moonrise over Earth's horizon from low orbit, and finally saw a passenger in the other seat. Not Petra—just a companion for the journey. Maybe the first time I'd really considered not being alone forever.

I listened to all of Side Two with the Silhouette in my hands—rolling it, flying it, letting it barrel-roll through my imaginary sky to the delight of whoever sat beside me. It was fun. I was happy.

I did see Petra again before she moved, but we didn't talk—at least not about anything important. Word must've gotten out about us on the dance floor; our parents kept us apart. Her mom vanished again—back to the Haight, I imagined, to join the forever-protests against Vietnam. My parents kept arguing. A growth spurt hurt. The Silhouette went back to my dresser, the Camaro to my desk, and the rest into a carrier—never to be seen again until I unearthed them at my mom's house half a century later.

I know what you're thinking: why sell a car with so much emotional weight—especially for a measly fifty bucks? Simple. The memories weren't because of the cars; the cars were just the backdrop to growing up. Writing these stories and sharing them affected me more than staring at a toy on a shelf and watching my childhood gather dust. I know these cars didn't go to romantic little kids with notions of spaceflight—some collector with ten already probably bought this one. But maybe, just maybe, someone visiting that die-cast shrine will see the Silhouette—my Silhouette—and be momentarily propelled into orbit to admire the rising moon and the setting sun.

Maybe they'll have someone with them.

Hopefully, they'll be happy.

Photo Credit Emily J Parent

Dan's desired life goals of being a professional layabout and part-time man-about-town were interrupted when he accidentally became a comic book publisher. Founding his comic book company, SLG Publishing in 1986,

 Dan went on to publish many eclectic and idiosyncratic titles such as *Johnny the Homicidal Maniac* by Jhonen Vasquez, *Lenore* by Roman Dirge, and a host of other creators and titles which are too numerous to mention. In addition to his publishing work, Dan briefly wrote for DC Comics, most notably producing a thankfully-forgotten-until-someone-decided-to-reprint-it run of *Justice League* comics at the same time as being one of the first writers published by DC Comics with a creator-owned contract with his series (with Norman Felchle), The Griffin.

Frequently travelling the path of most resistance, Dan founded a music venue called The Art Boutiki Music Hall. Opening in 2009 the Art Boutiki brought a combination of music, comics and other art all into one place until it closed in December of 2025. Dan can often be seen wandering the streets of Midtown in San Jose, walking up to people and saying, "Do you know who I AM?."

Today Dan hopes his experience co-hosting the podcast *The Unexpected Mentor* will land him some sort of job that does not require him to say "How's everything tasting tonight?"

www.slgpubs.com

graphic novels, books and more

www.ingramcontent.com/pod-product-compliance
Lightning Source LLC
Chambersburg PA
CBHW040322050426
42453CB00017B/2435